CREEPY *and* TRUE

BONES UNEARTHED!

KERRIE LOGAN HOLLIHAN

ABRAMS BOOKS FOR YOUNG READERS

NEW YORK

To Frederick William Holle
with my brightest hopes and dreams

Cataloging-in-Publication Data has been applied for and may be obtained from the Library of Congress.

ISBN 978-1-4197-5535-4

Text copyright © 2021 Kerrie Logan Hollihan
Edited by Howard W. Reeves
Book design by Becky James

For Picture Credits, see page 194.

Printed and bound in China

10 9 8 7 6 5 4 3 2

Abrams Books for Young Readers are available at special discounts when purchased in quantity for premiums and promotions as well as fundraising or educational use. Special editions can also be created to specification. For details, contact specialsales@abramsbooks.com or the address below.

ABRAMS The Art of Books
195 Broadway, New York, NY 10007
abramsbooks.com

CONTENTS

"Bones of All Men," circa 1520, from Hans Holbein's book, *The Dance of Death*. Skeletal trumpeters welcome the newly dead, as others wash bones in preparation for Judgment Day.

INTRODUCTION

Welcome to *Bones Unearthed!*

I started to think about this book quite some time ago. I envisioned it as a collection of tales about murder and about mayhem, which means disorder or chaos. "Cryptic* tales of murder and mayhem" is how I explain this project to my friends.

Truth be told, what follows are history lessons about remarkable, creepy, and true discoveries of skeletal remains. Bones of all sorts: crania, clavicles, femurs, fibulas, jaws, and more. Teeth, too, though they aren't bones, of course.

History? You might be thinking "Ugh. School."

Allow me a moment, please.

History tells tales about our past. Amazing true stories about all kinds of people and things that have come and gone since time began. Not only queens and kings and wars and such, but fantastic accounts of ordinary men, women, and children that are rich with details and show us how they

cryptic: with hidden meaning

lived. What is more, *their* lives and times tell us about *our* lives and times. A lesson that we should never forget!

You can think of historians as detectives doing an investigation. They ask a ton of questions:

Who?

What?

When?

Where?

Why?

And then later on . . . *how?*

And even later . . . *what if?*

So how does a writer of history go about investigating? That answer would be:

Research! In the course of writing this book, I did a boatload of exploring.

I made a virtual dig into the graves of all the people you will read about, and I ended up learning new things about old stuff I'd studied in school. The Russian Revolution, ancient China, Benjamin Franklin, earthquakes, and King Richard III of England. It turned out that every one of these topics was tangled up with murder, mayhem, or both . . . Creepy!

I had to learn about geology—what's gone on in the ground beneath our feet—and I'm not talking graves only.

I needed a refresher in biology, as well, specifically about deoxyribonucleic acid—what you and I refer to as DNA. I had never heard of it when I was your age. It was being studied in university by very bright professors, but DNA didn't make it into the daily newspapers until later in the 1980s. DNA is the material that carries all the information about how a living thing will look and function. It is in every cell of every living thing.

I needed to think about math, too. Here's an example:

> When I write that humans have walked the earth for about three hundred thousand years, I must put that in perspective and picture this fact in my mind. So I thought about my father, who died at nearly age one hundred.
>
> In my brain I compare three hundred thousand years to my dad's age:
>
> **300,000 v. 100**
>
> or
>
> **300,000 ÷ 100 = 3,000**
>
> Now I have the perspective I need. Humans have been around about three thousand times longer than the years my dad lived from 1920 until 2020. Let's take that thought one step further. If Dad's life was one American football field long—100 yards—then human existence stretches three thousand football fields!

I hope that you enjoy reading about and discovering these histories of bones as much as I have enjoyed learning and writing about them for YOU!

And, of course, they are all creepy and true.

RICARDVS · III · ANG · REX ·

King Richard III of England as he was pictured
by an unknown artist two hundred years after
he was killed on Bosworth Field

CHAPTER ONE

DIGGING ON THE BONES OF A KING

ON AUGUST 22, 1485, THERE WAS A BATTLE . . .

Mounted on his horse, King Richard Plantagenet stood ready to defend his honor and his crown. Across the no-name field near the hamlet of Bosworth waited his enemy, an upstart noble named Henry Tudor. Henry had his eyes on the prize; he wanted nothing less than to be king of England. It was a War of the Roses—white for the king's family, the House of York, and red for Henry's clan, the House of Lancaster. That day, their armies met on an open field. That day, they played the deadliest game of thrones ever.

A family feud, one might say.

Their families went into battle. Richard wore a circlet of gold around his helmet. It made him a marked man. The king's closest friends wore metal badges of wild pigs; Richard had picked out the white boar as his personal brand.

The king led the charge, sworn to slay his enemy and keep that golden circle on his helmet. But his hapless horse floundered in swampy ground, and he was forced to dismount. Richard, a fearsome fighter, swung his sword and battled alongside his men. His courage reigned when he refused their offer of a new mount to escape. And in the end, a red rose warrior planted a fatal blow across the back of Richard's head.

The victorious Lancastrians swept across the battleground to sort the dead and dying men of York. They celebrated not only victory, but the end of the Plantagenets, who never again ruled England. There on the battlefield, with the stink of blood and sweat, and tears all around, the golden circlet was placed on Henry's head. He became the seventh Henry and the first Tudor to rule England.

Richard's naked body was slung over a horse and paraded past cheering, jeering onlookers. Some poked it with their weapons, and one drove his sword into the pasty white skin of the dead king's buttock.

Eventually, someone did the decent thing and, with the horse as hearse, escorted the royal corpse to the monks at Grey Friar's Church in nearby Leicester (which rhymes with "pester"). The men of God whispered hasty prayers over the mutilated body. They dumped the dead king in an unmarked grave with neither coffin nor shroud to cradle his bones.

THE RUMORS SPREAD . . .

Once on the throne, the Tudors—five of them eventually ruled—badmouthed Richard III all over England. The blacker the stories about Richard Plantagenet, the better for Henry Tudor and his family. The Tudors, you see, stopped at nothing to make sure their power held. Heads rolled and flames burned high when they punished those—woman or man— who threatened them.

Their friends embarked on a course of creative writing. The stories claimed that Richard was ugly and had a crooked back, that his people hated him, and worst of all, that Richard had murdered his two little nephews so he could become king. The very best author was an actor named William Shakespeare, who told it

This playbill from 1884 shows actor Thomas W. Keene portraying the king in William Shakespeare's play *Richard III.*

all in 1597 in a mean-spirited play called *Richard III*. For generations, it has been performed wherever English is spoken (which is a big chunk of the planet), and kids have grown up thinking that Richard was an evil hunchback with a chip on his crooked shoulder.

THE FRIARY WENT MISSING . . .

In 1509 a new Henry, son of Henry VII, sat on England's throne. (You may know him as King Henry VIII, who had six wives—but not all at once.) This Henry despised monks because they forbade divorce, so they got in the way of his replacing Wife Number One with Wife Number Two. In revenge, he knocked down Grey Friars—the friary and its church—in Leicester in 1538. Its walls crumbled, and its bricks were carted off for new buildings and churches that Henry favored. The very church, as well as the monks' living quarters and sleeping spaces, went missing.

Poor dead Richard's grave was forgotten. But his body still lay there, as five hundred years of civilization piled on top of him. Five feet of civilization—dirt, bricks, stones, asphalt, broken bottles, trash—the usual junk that cities sit on.

FROM 1538–2012, THE MYSTERY LINGERED . . .

For 527 years, it stayed an unsolved mystery:

Where lay the body of King Richard the Third of England?

How did he die?

And was he the ugly, evil hunchback as the Tudors claimed?

THEN CAME THE DIG . . .

Five hundred years after Richard's death, Richard's fan club, once known as the Fellowship of the White Boar, demanded a search for the long-dead monarch. From Leicester to London and around the world, so-called Ricardians claimed that Richard Plantagenet had gotten a dirty deal. Naysayers scoffed at the idea, claiming that Richard's body was nowhere to be found. Some thought that when the church was knocked down, Richard's bones were thrown in the river.

It took decades, but eventually, the Ricardians raised enough cash to get things rolling. They had read the old histories and new research. Now they suspected that the old friary, along with Richard's grave, might be underground in the heart of Leicester between two buildings.

With the blessing of the Leicester city fathers, as well as a top-notch team of archaeologists and scientists from Leicester's very own university, the digging began. In Leicester, in a parking lot used by city workers. "A car park," as the English say. Which would be a dreary final resting place for anyone.

Did they guess correctly?

Did someone pave a grave and put up a parking lot?

Archaeologists begin their dig in a parking lot to search for the old Grey Friars church. A set of human bones was found where the "stickman" is lying.

Philippa Langley, a Scottish screenwriter with a passion for Richard's history, thought so.

> When you're writing a screenplay, you walk 1,000 miles in their shoes every day. I wasn't interested in Richard's death, I was interested in his life, but finally I thought I should go to Leicester—and the first time I stood in that car park, the strangest feeling just washed over me. I thought: "I am standing on Richard's grave." I came back again about a year later, thinking my earlier reaction was just nonsense, and the feeling was stronger than ever—only this time somebody had painted an R on a parking space.

Early on the morning of August 25, 2012, a small crowd gathered outside the parking lot at the locked gate to peer inside. Inside, it looked like an exploratory dig. A couple of workmen, with archaeologists and Ricardians (Richard's fan club) standing by.

A workman fired up a pavement cutter and sawed through a pair of bright yellow lines painted on the asphalt. A backhoe operator went to working, scraping away the blacktop to dig what would be a neat trench, Trench 1, five feet deep and thirty feet long. The foundations of one-hundred-year-old buildings appeared in the trench, but those weren't what everyone was looking for. The digging continued. There would be three trenches in all.

Then the digger unearthed a pair of leg bones about sixteen and one-half feet (five meters) from the north end of the trench and about five feet (one and one-half meters) underground. They lay parallel, signs of an "undisturbed burial," as an archaeologist would say, but no one could be sure if the legs belonged to a complete skeleton.

Medieval churches often housed burials, so the leg bones weren't a big surprise. The archaeologists stayed cool. One took some notes and then covered the bones back up. They couldn't just dig those leg bones out. No one knew if the two leg bones signified a burial or even if they had dug into a church. Bone removal was someone else's responsibility and needed an official permit.

As they waited, the archaeologists dug more. They found an old wall, built medieval-style, running from east to west, as well as part of a low stone wall a few feet away.

The long wall was "robbed," in archaeology-speak. When Grey Friars was knocked down in 1538, its bricks were carted away, probably to build other churches. Even the foundations were robbed, leaving long, ghostly channels behind. Over time these filled up with rubble, stones, and soil, leaving a gritty outline to mark exactly where Grey Friars stood.

More walls appeared, along with rows of squares stamped into the hard-packed earth. Tile floors, it seemed, would have lined the floor of a medieval church.

The next day the team finished digging Trench 1 and found a second robbed wall that was parallel to the one they found the day before. Then they dug Trench 2, also thirty meters long. There they found signs of a second building and a pair of stone benches, with more tile flooring in between. Aha! The monks of Grey Friars would have sat on these facing benches in their chapter house to visit. After all, there was no talking in church.

The whole next week, they kept digging, still waiting to apply for a permit to study the area around those leg bones. On Friday August 31, the investigators applied for an official permit to exhume (remove) up to six sets of human remains from the site. As everyone knows, the government can take its time.

On Saturday they dug Trench 3, thirty meters long as well. It exposed two more walls that ran east to west

[Two] walls ... match up, meaning that the human remains found on the first day ... lie inside the eastern half of the church, quite possibly the choir—where Richard III was reputedly buried.

The archaeologists had uncovered solid evidence that a friary once stood at the site, home to monks and priests who wore the dun-colored robes of the Gray Friars. In other words, the archaeologists felt sure they'd dug into a church.

On Tuesday, September 4, the archaeologists held the government permit in their hands. A digger widened the spot where that pair of leg bones had first appeared, giving everyone, including the skeleton, more elbow room.

THE RESEARCHERS DROPPED IN ...

Another archaeologist and a scientist arrived, both masked women dressed from head to ankles in protective white suits. One was Dr. Jo Appleby, an osteoarchaeologist who focuses on studying old bones. The other was Dr. Turi King, a geneticist who specializes in excavating ancient remains under clean conditions and then extracting DNA from the ancient remains.

They worked slowly, pulling away the hard soil with trowels. None of their own DNA, not even a sneeze, could contaminate the site. "We excavated his legs up to his pelvis and then because, with a film crew there, we would never get the skeleton lifted that day and couldn't leave it exposed, we left him covered ready for the next day," Dr. King explained. They had discovered something odd. His feet were missing!

Not until the next day did Appleby work her way farther around the skeleton, exposing the legs and uncovering pelvic bones. The pelvis confirmed she was excavating a male.

Then it dawned on everyone that they weren't working in a typical grave, which would be long and rectangular. This one looked bath-shaped and wasn't finished off at the sides.

Osteoarchaeologist Dr. Jo Appleby excavates the human bones brought to light during the dig.

Could this be a sign? Had the grave diggers cut a smaller hole than usual to bury this body quickly?

Dr. Appleby excavated a different place and found a skull in an odd spot. Instead of lying flat, it lay chin to chest so that the top of the skull was higher in the grave than expected. The skull faced left and downward, as if the man wanted to look at his own dead bones. It seemed his corpse was crammed into its final resting place, another clue that this grave was dug in a hurry.

The skull told them more. Clearly, it bore the marks of battle wounds.

Appleby then unearthed the skeleton's arms and rib cage. She also noted what was missing—any sign of a coffin or even shreds of a shroud. After all, bodies in shrouds normally have their collarbones shoved up to their ears—thanks to being wrapped so tightly. Here was more evidence that the man hadn't gotten a proper burial.

Except for the wind, all was quiet as the scientist worked her small tool around the pelvis to locate the base of the skeleton's spine. She cleared away soil along its vertebrae and was astonished to find the pieces following an S-shape. This was the backbone of a man with a deformity.

Legend said that King Richard had a twisted spine.

By nightfall each bone was tagged and bagged. Three—the skull, the lower jaw, and one femur—were wrapped in aluminum foil to keep clean. The bones were whisked away for safekeeping and further study.

The bones of a man with a twisted spine lay uncovered after resting for centuries in an unmarked grave.

Along with the skeleton, the findings also had led to the discovery of the church itself and the chapter house. There the monks had shared their meals and sat face-to-face on a pair of stone benches to chat—when talking was allowed. Friaries and monasteries are usually quiet places. But if the body of a murdered king had arrived? Life might have been noisy for a while. And surely the monks would have had lots to talk about.

What was more, the dig revealed that the bones were buried in an honored spot within the church. Whoever was boss at Grey Friars had placed the grave just inside a doorway between two sections of the church. Right where the monks would walk over them, day in and day out, presumably for centuries.

Dr. Richard Buckley, the lead archaeologist at the University of Leicester, explained why. "It's considered that burials were often placed where people would walk over them because it adds impact to them [the buried dead] . . . and increases the sort of reverence . . ." But as we now know, the church was knocked down only fifty-three years later.

THE WAIT TO IDENTIFY THE BONES WENT ON . . .

A shroud of secrecy surrounded the project. The team had collected bits of evidence that seemed to fall in place like puzzle pieces. They found a friary and its church. They dug out a misshapen grave inside the church in an honored spot. They excavated a skeleton with a curved spine and battle marks on its skull.

But this wasn't Hollywood, and studying the bones would take far longer than what you'd see on a television show.

On Friday, September 14, three weeks after the dig started, the archaeologists spread a protective film over their exposed finds and filled them by hand with soil. The digger backfilled Trenches 1, 2, and 3, and it was back to business as usual aboveground. The archaeologists' paradise went back to being a parking lot.

MEANWHILE, AT LEICESTER UNIVERSITY . . .

Dr. Appleby, the bone archaeologist, noted that the skull had a number of interesting characteristics, and they learned a lot more as they analyzed it.

> . . . there were several glancing blows really from a sharp implement that had taken small quantities of bone off the surface of the skull. We also identified a penetrating wound on top of the skull. This was caused by something that had been brought down on top of the head with enough force that it actually dislodged two flaps of bone on the bone interior.
>
> There was also a much larger wound on the base of the skull and in this case a whole portion of bone appeared to have been cleaved off with a very sharp blade perhaps something along the lines of a halberd [a combined spear and battle-axe] which is something that we know was often used during medieval warfare and depending on precisely how far the blade penetrated into the skull it could have caused death instantaneously.
>
> So we do have at least one wound that is a very good candidate for being fatal.

Once the researchers spent more time with the bones, they decided that there were two wounds that could have killed this man. It seems curious that the skull's face had only minor injuries. Intentional, explained Dr. Appleby. "[Henry] was able to show that Richard actually was dead."

They also discovered a blade had also punched through the hip bone, the pelvis.

When Appleby studied the vertebrae, she concluded that this person had suffered from scoliosis. The spine had started its painful curve sideways during the victim's teenage years.

🏛 🏛 🏛

Dr. Turi King, meanwhile, took on the task of finding out whether a tooth in the skull could provide DNA for her to study.

The skull, lower jaw, and femur of the mystery man rested in a special room. There Dr. King unwrapped the jawbone, took it in her gloved hand, and started wiggling teeth. She found "the wiggliest," gave it a tug, and *voilà*, out popped the tooth, root and all. (A molar, the back M3, to be precise.)

For a tooth that has been buried for 527 years, it looked remarkably undamaged. But did it hold ancient DNA? Mitochondrial DNA, the kind that's passed from mothers to their sons and daughters down through the generations?

If the answer was yes, that would be huge. But there was one more hurdle. Would that DNA match someone from Richard III's family?

Two samples of royal Plantagenet mitochondrial DNA were on hand. One had come from Wendy Duldig, a living female descendent of Richard's older sister, Anne of York.

The other came from Duldig's fourteenth cousin, twice removed, a Canadian named Michael Ibsen who lived in England. His mother had descended from Anne, too. A

DNA sample came from a few cells swabbed inside his cheek. Michael Ibsen knew he was related to Richard, but Wendy Duldig, born in Australia, had had no idea until a researcher called her and the test took place.

THE SCIENTISTS HELD THEIR BREATH . . .

Dr. King talked about the process of looking for DNA in the tooth:

> You grind up the sample into a powder and you put that powder into a tube, but whilst

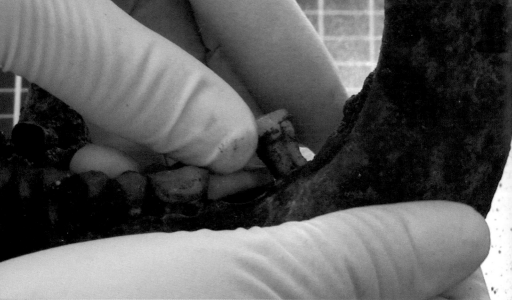

Geneticist Dr. Turi King gently pulls a molar from the jaw of the unidentified man.

**you're running all of this . . . you run two
blank tubes either side of that.**

King added these sample tubes—there's no DNA in them—to help prove her test results are accurate.

**Now what you're hoping is that
at the end of this process . . . you only
get DNA out of the one that had the tooth
powder in and not out of the blanks.**

**And that's exactly what happened. We
found the blanks were empty, and the only
DNA we had came from the tooth.**

Sure enough, there was DNA in that molar. King was delighted. Mitochondrial DNA in the mystery molar had held together well enough for her to study. Enough DNA for even more lab tests, with pages and pages of impressive results.

And they all confirmed one thing: That molar had the very same mitochondrial DNA as Wendy Duldig and Michael Ibsen.

THE VERDICT IS READ . . .

On February 4, 2013, media reps from all over the world gathered at a news conference at Leicester University. For more than half an hour, they listened silently as the historians, archaeologists, and scientists made their case:

- A church had been discovered.
- A hastily dug grave had been located in a prominent spot.
- The grave held a male skeleton, not fully extended, with an S-curved spine.
- Radiocarbon dating of the bones linked them to the time when Richard was alive.
- Mitochondrial DNA from the tooth showed a match with descendants of the Plantagenet Royals.

On the left is Michael Ibsen, a modern member of Richard III's family line. Professor Caroline Wilkinson of the Liverpool School of Art and Design produced the model of Richard's face from a 3D scan of the skull. Do you see a resemblance?

The experts delivered their verdict:

> Ladies and gentlemen, it is the academic
> conclusion of the University of Leicester
> that beyond reasonable doubt the individual
> exhumed at Greyfriars on September 2012 is
> indeed Richard III, the last Plantagenet
> king of England.

People in the crowd sat quiet a moment, and then smiles broke out amid a few whoops of congratulations. Reporters picked up their phones, and satellite images zipped around the world. For those in the history business, the science business, and the royal business, it was a remarkable discovery.

And quite lucky, the experts added. The king's skeleton probably lost its feet when some Victorians built themselves an outhouse only inches west of him. What happened to Richard's foot bones, then?

Disturbing, indeed.

THE SORRY SAGA OF THE LITTLE PRINCES

Did a sinister Richard III order the murder of his two young nephews in the Tower of London? The boys disappeared after the death of their father, Edward IV. Twelve-year-old Edward V (or so he would have been) and nine-year-old Richard, Duke of York, were living in the Tower of London before Edward V was to be crowned.

It was expected that young Edward would become king, but his uncle Richard usurped England's throne. Richard justified his power grab by saying that Edward's father and mother weren't married under England's law, which made the boys illegitimate. Yet Richard's claim was pretty much bogus, too.

First the brothers were seen at the Tower, and then they were not. The rumors spread that Richard had done them in so that he could become king.

And then the bones of two boys were discovered in the Tower in 1674 and were thought to be those of Edward V and his brother Richard. They were encased in a marble urn in England's grand cathedral, Westminster Abbey. All this time, those bones have stayed officially unidentified, and the mystery has lingered.

Sir John Edward Millais painted this tender image, *The Two Princes Edward and Richard in the Tower*, in 1878, long after they disappeared.

We think that the murder story was cooked up by one Sir Thomas More to bolster the Tudor family's claim to the throne. (King Henry VIII later beheaded Sir Thomas when Henry wanted a divorce. But

Sir Thomas, representing the Catholic Church, said no. Henry got his divorce, and Thomas became a saint. You can see how truth is stranger than fiction.)

Seventy years on, we still don't know for sure what happened to the little princes.

From the looks of things, there will be no DNA testing of any boy's bones in Westminster Abbey anytime soon. The abbey said so, as did Her Royal Majesty Queen Elizabeth II, who is supreme governor of the Church of England.

FACTLET

A FAMILY SECRET

MORE DNA TESTS ON Richard's bones turned up another surprise. This time, the experts looked at the Y chromosomes in his male family DNA. They discovered at least one break in the family DNA, a chain along the male line that's nineteen links long. "A false paternity event," it's called. In other words, at least one lady along the royal Richard's family line was having a jolly time with someone other than her husband, and so her boy child was not his.

CHAPTER TWO

STONES AND BONES ... KRAKATOA AND TAMBORA

BEFORE WE BEGIN . . . CHECK OUT THE MAPS ON THE
FACING PAGE TO FIND A FEW SPOTS:

- Tanzania (once called Zanzibar) in East Africa
- Indonesia, due east across the Indian Ocean from Tanzania
- On the bottom map, look for Krakatoa, also called Anak Krakatau or Rakata Island in Indonesia. There are many names for this volcano and the island, which is in fact an active volcano. Krakatoa is in the Sunda Strait that separates the islands of Java and Sumatra.

Now you have a mind map of what you will read next . . .

🏛 🏛 🏛

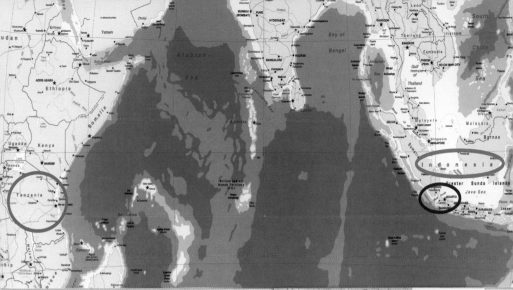

The green circle (above) shows Tanzania/Zanzibar. The orange oval denotes Indonesia and the red oval shows the location of the Sunda Strait and Krakatau (Krakatoa).

The Sunda Strait sits between the islands of Sumatra and Java in Indonesia.

On a Sunday morning in 1884, a grown-up at a mission school in Tanzania (once two territories, one called Zanzibar) in east Africa took a group of boys for a walk on the beach. A fierce storm the night before had littered the beach with debris swept in by the Indian Ocean. Oceans do that all the time, but on this day, the beach had a creepy-ish feel.

The school headmistress wrote a long letter to the Royal Society, the hallowed group of scientists in England.

About the third week in July 1884, the boys ... were much amused by finding on

the beach stone which would float, evidently
pumice stone. The lady who was with them
... also noticed that there were a quantity of
human skulls and bones "all along the beach
at high-water mark"; these were quite clean
and had no flesh remaining on them, and
we found at intervals of a few yards, two
or three lying close together.

In 2003 a geologist-turned-author named Simon
Winchester had this to say in his book *Krakatoa* about that
peculiar pumice with stones and bones:

Welded thickly on to the rock's upper
surface and giving it the most macabre
appearance were dozens of human skeletons,
together with the bones of monkeys and,
distinguishable only later in the day when
the school biology teacher had appeared, the
skeletons of a pair of big cats, most probably
Sumatran tigers.

The bones on the beach were remains from a disaster
that had taken place *five thousand five hundred miles* (seven
thousand three hundred kilometers) away and *eleven months
earlier.* The raft of rock had floated west to the east coast
of Africa. Its origin: a volcano on an island far to the east
in Indonesia, about one-fourth of the distance around the
earth. Its name was Krakatoa.

On Saturday morning, August 26, 1883, this Krakatoa volcano on the island of Rakata exploded. Six cubic miles (twenty-one cubic kilometers) of pyroclastic flow—ash, pumice, and 1,000°F gas (that's 538°C)— blasted into the stratosphere. Rakata seems to have been uninhabited, no people living there. And yet, a series of four explosions from that Saturday morning until 10 A.M. Sunday would affect people around the world.

This lithograph from 1888 depicts Krakatoa's explosion in 1883.

At 2 P.M. on Saturday, the ash plume shot seventeen miles (twenty-seven kilometers) skyward. By Sunday night, the plume had soared fifty miles (eighty kilometers). When the dust settled later, the volcano was gone. Two-thirds of surrounding land was, too. The massive explosion created a shock wave in the atmosphere. This shockwave circled the planet *seven times*.

Explosions. Shock waves. And associated with them to create even more danger: tsunamis, fast-moving waves that swept across the sea creating gigantic one-hundred-foot-high (thirty meters) walls of water. These catastrophically destroyed one hundred sixty-five villages all on Java and Sumatra. Working as one, all of these took their toll on human life. Most of the human victims died by drowning.

As the explosions came, one by one, lava (called magma below earth's surface) gushed through the hole in the seabed. Volcanic gases dissolved in the magma expand rapidly when the lava reaches the surface of the earth. These expanding gases create a froth full of vesicles—gas bubbles—that in ocean water cool and quickly solidify into pumice, a light-weight and abrasive volcanic rock. (People can use pumice stones to smooth rough spots on their feet.)

Some pumice was small in size, but other pieces fused into thick floating rafts of rock, rare and spectacular. This fusion process picked up any debris in the water at that time, including debris the tsunamis had washed into the sea, from barnacles to trees to bones of animals—and of people.

STONES AND BONES ... KRAKATOA AND TAMBORA

Krakatoa had an early-warning system. In May it had begun spewing ash to a six-mile (ten-kilometer) height. Now on that fateful weekend in late August, people in Batavia (now Jakarta, Indonesia) heard the volcano rumble. They lived one hundred miles (one hundred sixty kilometers) away. They heard it in Perth on the west coast of Australia, too—one thousand nine hundred miles (three thousand kilometers) away.

The *New York Times* reported that sailors in faraway ships heard cannonades (cannon fire) off in the distance. People in Singapore were choked by a pungent dust so fine that it filtered through mosquito nets. On Monday morning in Batavia on Java, everyone awoke in total darkness. If they ventured outside, they breathed tainted air and fainted. So they barred their doors, to sit and wait.

The *Times* continued:

. . . And now tidings of disaster began to come thick and fast from every side. Miles of flourishing plantations had been blasted by the burning ashes, and the labors of years were destroyed in one night. The sea, shaken to its lowest depths, rose and fell like a fountain jet, flinging boats and even large ships up on the shore. Neither chart nor compass could save their bewildered seamen, who, voyaging over perfectly familiar waters, found sea in the place of land and land in the place of sea. In Batavia itself the streets were heaped with volcanic ashes and lava dust, while a succession of mountain waves, bursting upon the shore, rendered any approach from that side impossible.

But worse was still to come . . .

Three good-sized towns on nearby islands—Anjer, Tjeringen, and Teluk Betong—were gone. There were tales of townspeople clawing their way up hillsides only to be dragged down by frantic folk below them. Observers on ships watched as tsunamis washed over towns on the coast. One man, rescued by ship, was the sole survivor in his village.

But stories of survival were rare. Most people died— choked by volcanic gas, smothered in tephra (volcanic rock fragments), or drowned in the sweeping walls of water one hundred twenty feet (thirty-seven meters) high.

An eyewitness to the horror told his story in 1890. On that Saturday, August 26, a Dutch water engineer named R. A. van Sandick boarded the steamer *Gouverneur-Generaal Loudon* to take a new job on the island of Sumatra. Van Sandick was aboard with about one hundred others.

The *Loudon* set sail from the city of Batavia in the morning. It was to call at several ports on the island of Sumatra along the way: Betong, Kroë, Benkoelen, Padang, and Aceh.

As they sailed, Krakatoa blew. That night the *Loudon*'s captain, T. H. Lindemann, spotted a tsunami heading their

This painting depicts a search party looking at the bones of once living things killed by the Krakatoa eruption. They are shown carrying live chickens to test for poison gas coming from the ground. The birds would pass out or die from the fumes ahead of the humans, and the search party would then be able to move away to safety.

way and pointed his ship directly at the wave. The *Loudon* rose and fell as the tsunami swept underneath.

From the deck van Sandick witnessed the devastation all over Sumatra and more. The *Loudon* returned to Batavia, only to find that it, too, was gone. His words, roughly translated from Dutch, capture the hopelessness:

> Many of the 12,500 victims in Sumatra have been washed out to sea. But thousands of bodies remained on the coast. The population of that part of Sumatra is scarce and the means of community [help] are difficult. Weeks after the devastation of the coastal lands, [they] seem to be rotting unburied, lay on the coast, spreading a horrible air and filling the atmosphere with miasmas [a stink or stench].

"Seem to be rotting unburied . . ." In the warm, tropical climate, the bodies were decomposing from flesh to bones.

At the time, scientists said ". . . this immense chain of volcanic mountains [across Java and Sumatra] points to the existence of a great fissure [a long crack] in the earth's crust, along which the subterranean energy has been manifested . . ." It would take ninety years more for scientists to "see" the suspected fissure using sonar technology.

When Krakatoa erupted, word of the disaster spread swiftly. At that time continents were connected by networks of telegraph cables strung along the ocean floor. When Krakatoa made its grand finale on Sunday night, August 26, newspapers ran the story within hours.

In *Krakatoa*, Winchester described a terrible scene:

> **The first terse signal—The first "Strong volcanic eruption, Krakatoa Island"—from the Lloyd's agent [a businessman] who saw the flames spout from the volcano's summit, was carried over lines that were almost immediately broken by the tsunami that killed 36,000 people a few seconds later.**

Thirty-six thousand people.

🏛 🏛 🏛

Mother Nature also told the world about the Krakatoa disaster, though not quite as fast. Around the globe that year, vivid sunrises and sunsets of red and orange caught the public's attention. "A remarkable atmospheric phenomenon," "great brilliancy," and "afterglow" all were descriptions in *Science* magazine the next January.

Some believed that earth's travel through "meteoric dust" contributed to these events, but an astronomer at Brown University, Dr. Winslow Upton, insisted that Krakatoa also had played a part. "It is impossible not to conjecture a connection with a volcanic eruption in the Sunda Strait, by which, on August 26th, the island of Krakatoa disappeared wholly from the face of the earth."

The sky's brilliance inspired poets, authors, and artists. Best known among all their work is *The Scream*, an iconic painting. Its Norwegian artist, Edvard Munch, took in the sight on an end-of-day walk with friends under a "blood red" sky.

> ... Clouds like blood and tongues of fire hung above the blue-black fjord and the city. My friends went on, and I stood alone, trembling with anxiety. I felt a great, unending scream piercing through nature.

🏛 🏛 🏛

Ten years later Munch put that memory on canvas. That great unending scream unnerved me when I saw it in a German museum back in my high school days. Even now, when I think of that image, all I envision is that creepy face that Munch painted. Only as I was writing this book did I

The Scream by Edvard Munch, 1893

learn that the painting could be linked to the Krakatoa eruption.

To me, the subject in *The Scream* looked only like skin on a skull.

🏠 🏠 🏠

Does it surprise you that Krakatoa still speaks? In 1928 a new volcanic cone started to rise from the sea about a three-minute walk away from where Krakatoa blew. It is named Anak Krakatoa, the "child of Krakatoa." Like its mighty ancestor, it erupted in 2018. It appears that this volcanic child generated a rockslide under the sea and a tsunami that killed hundreds of people in Java, I am sorry to say.

In a manner of speaking, Krakatoa is "living on the edge." Geologists explain that it sits where an ocean plate and a land plate meet.

As an ocean plate (extraordinarily slowly) slides under a land plate, the ocean plate bends under the edge of the land plate. It's there, where the two plates come together, that volcanos rise and magma, hot liquid rock, comes to the surface.

In 1996, geologist Keith Kirk visited Indonesia and saw gigantic ejecta blocks from the original eruption that are still present on the beach. In the far distance, Anak Krakatau smoked and boomed every twenty to thirty minutes.

Krakatoa was formed as the Indo-Australian plate, an oceanic plate, slid under the Eurasian plate. It sat quiet for centuries on top of a pressure cooker of magma. In time—a very long time—the shifting earth created a hole in the ocean floor and Krakatoa erupted ash, magma, gases, pumice ... you name it.

And now you understand how and why that pumice raft with human bones landed on the beach in Zanzibar nine months after Krakatoa erupted. That raft of rock had floated nearly straight west from Indonesia.

Author's note: As I scrolled through Twitter on Friday night, April 10, 2020, I read that Anak Krakatoa had blown yet again. Volcanos are true to their nature. Creepy as well.

WHAT LIES BENEATH A LONDON MARKET?

In the 1990s a vast mass grave was discovered under a busy marketplace in East London, England. Archaeologists from the Museum of London launched a sixteen-year project to study the whys and wherefores at the site, because it housed more than ten thousand five hundred skeletons. At first

FACTLET

KRAKATOA THE CALDERA

AT FIRST IT SEEMED that Krakatoa had blown itself into oblivion. But geologists (most but not all) eventually agreed that it had collapsed, forming a caldera.

Yet after geologists studied the rock and ash that dropped on islands all over the region, they discovered that only ten percent of it was from the original volcanic cone. The rest was new material, magma that had blown through the cone and cooled off into pumice and ash. The mighty Krakatoa hadn't truly blown apart. Instead, it sank into the ocean and formed a caldera.

A caldera is a wide, bowl-shaped depression, what's left after a chamber of boiling hot magma bursts through Earth's crust. Calderas, in fact, take their name from the Spanish word for "cauldron."

Anak Krakatoa, meaning "child of Krakatoa," rises from the water near where Krakatoa first erupted.

Once that chamber empties out, down comes everything above and around it. And so a caldera is born.

Only part of Krakatoa had jutted out above the sea. The rest of the volcano had sat under the ocean inside another caldera. This caldera, four miles (twelve kilometers) wide, was formed after an even older (like one million years old) volcano had exploded centuries before. (If you are now picturing a bowl within a bowl, you'd be right.)

it seemed the dead had died of bubonic plague or famine that visited England in the 1300s and 1400s. The place was known as Spitalfields.

But then: SURPRISE! Don Walker, an osteologist (bone specialist) at the museum, went public with his ideas. Walker and other researchers had studied the bones from a number of graves. They tweaked an old research tool, radiocarbon dating, and estimated them to be about eight hundred fifty years old.

Walker believed that many of the dead people buried at Spitalfields were the eventual, ultimate victims of a cataclysmic volcano that erupted in 1258 AD. We don't know when, nor where, but Walker declared that this eruption dwarfed Krakatoa by eight times the amount of "stuff" blown skyward. He based his ideas on evidence of ash buried deep in ice in spots all around the world.

It's likely that this mass grave discovered under a busy shopping area in London is linked to the Tambora explosion.

A monk at work in a monastery in St. Albans, England, nearly eight hundred years ago also helped Walker to make the connection. The monk was one Matthew Paris, and he left a rich account of local life in the 1250s in *Historia Anglorum*.

It's possible that ash from the mystery volcano blocked sunlight and warmth. Paris talked of the bitter cold in England in 1258 that forbade spring planting and took its toll on the poor:

. . . when April, May, and the principal part of June, had

passed, and scarcely were there visible any of the small

and rare plants, or any shooting buds of flowers; and, in consequence, but small hopes were entertained of the fruit crops. Owing to the scarcity of wheat, a very large number of poor people died; and dead bodies were found in all directions, swollen and livid, lying by fives and sixes in pigsties, on dunghills, and in the muddy streets . . . When several corpses were found, large and spacious holes were dug in the cemeteries, and a great many bodies were laid in them together.

Mathew Paris was writing about mass graves, a practical solution when the living must bury an overwhelming number of the dead.

In the 1250s these were bodies. By the 2000s they were bones.

THE YEAR WITHOUT A SUMMER

At year's end in 1816, a New Hampshire man—like Mathew Paris in 1259—remarked about the weather:

This past summer and fall have been so cold and miserable that I have from despair kept no account of the weather. It could have been nothing but a repeatation [sic] of frost and drought.

All over New England that year, folks thought the same. The year 1816 had been a year of weirdness, but no one knew why. Spring opened as usual, but icy cold then blasted buds on trees and froze seedlings in farmers' fields. In June it snowed. There were ice storms in July. The corn crop died, and with no corn to eat, cows died. By summer's end—if anyone could call it summer—many had left New England to make new lives in Indiana and Ohio, where the weather looked better. (In time they'd learn that life was just as tough in the Midwest.)

Carbonized bones from Tambora reveal what happened to those who lived nearby.

Across the Atlantic in Europe, the summer of 1816 was oddly rainy and cold, but Europeans had no explanation for that either. Central Europe saw the worst of that summer, especially people in Switzerland, whose crops were so poor that some resorted to eating cats.

The weather change also affected Southeast Asia. Regular rainy seasons, the monsoons, were thrown off and disrupted daily life. Many went hungry. In 1817 people in India fell sick, notably to cholera, a bacterial disease carried by drinking water contaminated by fecal matter (a nice way of saying that germ-laden poop was in their food supply). This cholera bacterium infected British soldiers, who took it aboard ship when they went home to England. From there, this deadly strain of cholera went to Europe and North America and made millions of people sick.

Today we know part of the "why" behind the Year Without a Summer: a volcano.

In 1815 Mount Tambora, also seated along the Indonesian archipelago, erupted. The explosion was beyond massive, blasting fifty cubic meters (thirty-six cubic miles) into the sky, *three times more* than when Krakatoa followed in 1883. As with Krakatoa, there had been an early warning system of hanging clouds and distant rumbles. The man charged with investigating Mount Tambora left early in April to check things out. He never came back.

About 7 P.M. on the 10th of April [1815], three distinct columns of flame burst forth near the top of Tomboro [Tambora] Mountain, all of them apparently within the verge of the Crater, and after ascending separately to a very great height, their tops united in the air in a troubled confused manner. In a short time the whole Mountain next Saugur [Sangar] appeared like a body of liquid fire extending itself in every direction.

The fire and columns of flame continued to rage with unabated fury until the darkness, caused by the quantity of falling matter, obscured it at about 8 p.m. Stones at this time fell very thick at Saugur—some of them as large as two fists, but generally not larger than walnuts; between 9 and 10 P.M. ashes began to fall, and soon after a violent whirlwind ensued, which blew down nearly every house in the village of Saugur, carrying the tops and light parts away with it.

In other places, the volcano did even more damage. This eyewitness account came from the Raja, the ruler, of Sanggar, whose small kingdom survived the explosion but lost many of its people.

In the part of Saugur adjoining Tomboro, its effects were much more violent, tearing up by the roots the largest trees, and carrying them into the air together with men, houses, cattle, and whatever else came within its influence (this will account for the immense number of floating trees seen at sea). The sea rose nearly twelve feet higher than it had ever been known to be before, and completely spoiled the only small spots of rice lands in Saugur—sweeping away houses and everything within its reach.

Two other princedoms, Pekat and Tambora, simply disappeared. The Tambora language was never to be spoken or heard again.

Bones might well tell the tale of this massive eruption. In 2004 archaeologist Dr. Haraldur Sigurdsson and researchers from the University of North Carolina and the Indonesian Directorate of Volcanology dug into the ground at Tambora and excavated a dwelling, thanks to ground-penetrating radar. Inside were all the signs of home—pots, tools, decorative ware, and more. And people—the carbonized bones of a woman and a man, their skeletons turned to charcoal from the volcano's mighty heat.

"She was knocked over on her back by the force of the pyroclastic flow, and she appeared to be holding a machete or long knife in one hand. Over her arm was a cloth, and we think it was a sarong, totally carbonized, and her body was extensively carbonized, too," Dr. Sigurdsson said. "Pyroclastic flow is rather like a snow avalanche. It's

People crowded in a boathouse in Herculaneum died when Mount Vesuvius erupted.

composed of particles of ash and pumice and gas—but at a thousand degrees—that moves at a high velocity, perhaps up to one hundred miles per hour."

It's possible, Dr. Sigurdsson added, that the entire area underground could be "the Pompei of the East," likening the Tambora site to the discovery of Pompei, Italy. Pompei, a thriving town southeast of modern-day Naples, was buried after Mount Vesuvius erupted in 79 AD. About two thousand people, not to mention their dogs and cats, perished as the volcano spewed ash, pumice, pyroclastic flows, and more from nineteen to twenty-three feet (six to seven meters) deep. Pompei lay hidden until 1748 when archaeologists nosed around the area and began to excavate. Immense heat from Vesuvius had *instantly* transformed living creatures into gray, ash-like sculptures. To see these dead in such natural poses is mind-bending.

Vesuvius had dumped harder material on Herculaneum, about ten miles (nineteen kilometers) away, to a depth of fifty to sixty feet (fifteen to eighteen meters). This debris hardened so that it preserved and protected the forgotten city from vandals and looters until archaeologists arrived in 1738 to start to explore. Only by chance had anyone discovered the city in 1709, when someone digging a well shoveled into an ancient theater.

For many years, it looked as if townspeople in Herculaneum had escaped the town and Vesuvius's wrath— until 1980, which is rather recent in archaeological terms. The bones of one hundred twenty people were discovered. Likely they died from *nuées ardentes,* French for "glowing cloud," what scientists would call "pyroclastic flow."

🏠 🏠 🏠

It's thought that the Mount Tambora eruption killed about one hundred seventeen thousand people. Some died outright from the blast, others drowned, and still others starved to death when volcanic ash blanketed their rice fields. People were so hungry that they ate horses and dogs. Families sold themselves into slavery in order to eat. It's been written that parents killed their children because they could not feed them.

The volcano had blown twenty-five miles into the stratosphere. The blast captured droplets of sulfur dioxide that developed into a fine mist called volcanic aerosol (think of hair spray, only toxic). In the coming months, the aerosol floated through the atmosphere and partly blocked the sun's radiation. Though widely dispersed around the earth, it didn't change the weather everywhere. But where solar radiation was veiled, temps were cooler. People in Europe and North America had no clue why their summers were so miserable.

In rain-soaked Switzerland, a small group of trendy English poets and their ladies gathered for summer vacation. Instead of blue skies and mountain walks, they were shut inside. An older man, the famed poet Lord Byron, challenged the others to write the scariest stories possible. Certainly, the oddly cold, gloomy days added inspiration. One young woman, the eighteen-year-old Mary Shelley, took up the challenge. It took her only a short while to pen (literally) a novel about a doctor who builds a living being from human parts. The doctor narrates his disrespectful body building, "I collected bones from charnel houses and disturbed . . . the tremendous secrets of the human frame."

Shelley's book took the world by storm. Its title was *Frankenstein*.

In Ireland crops of potatoes and wheat failed. Food became wildly expensive for poor families, and many grew weak from hunger. An epidemic "fever" began its run through Ireland, which we now call *typhus*, a bacterial disease.

A doctor noticed that poor country people had a better chance of surviving typhus than wealthier families. In towns people stayed close together in the same home when someone was sick even though the sick person might stay in a different room. It was easy for the bacteria to spread. But in the country, people with typhus were isolated from others, cast out to small "fever huts" receiving food and medicine from the end of a shovel or a pitchfork. They either died or got better.

The frontispiece of *Frankenstein*, the novel written in 1818 by Mary Shelley

There is much more to discover on Tambora. Dr. Sigurdsson told National Public Radio ". . . we've got lots of time. It's taken three hundred years to excavate Pompeii, and it's still not done, so we're in no hurry here either. We've got to leave something to be done by our grandchildren as well, so as to keep them busy."

Finding more bones in Tambora could well be up to you.

FACTLET

PLATE TECTONICS

EARTH'S CRUST, BOTH LAND and ocean floor, is broken into massive "plates" that slide in slow motion—like an inch (two and a half centimeters) per year. They never stop. Geologists call this process "plate tectonics." Understanding plate tectonics can be a lot to digest. To start, you need a mental view of earth's outer layers:

- Earth's very thin top layer is the *lithosphere*. We call it earth's crust.

- The lithosphere floats, we might say, atop the *asthenosphere*. The asthenosphere is the warm, melty outermost layer of the Earth's mantle. It's hot down there, and the closer to Earth's core, the hotter the mantle gets.

- There are fifteen tectonic plates floating on the asthenosphere. If you live on a continent, it sits on a huge plate. But if your house is in the Caribbean or on the Arabian Peninsula, that plate is much smaller.

Plate tectonics plays a mighty role in forming volcanos.

Author's note: When I was in school, "plate tectonics" wasn't a thing. The ocean bottom was being mapped with sonar technology, but the complete map wasn't published until 1977. Once geologists laid eyes on it, they finally grasped how the plates fit together on land and under the sea to create an enormous puzzle of pieces in never-ending motion.

Nor could I have imagined that plate tectonics would eventually, if slowly, lead archaeologists to finding volcanic bones. Or be on my plate to study, as well.

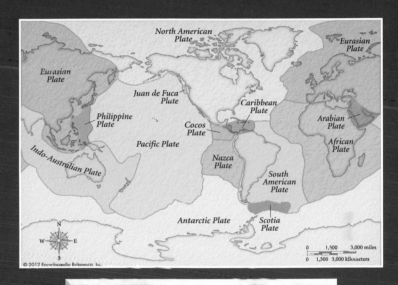

There are seven major and eight minor tectonic plates around the globe.

CHAPTER THREE

DE-ICING THE FRANKLIN EXPEDITION— DOWN TO THE BONES

A WHILE BACK, I CAME ACROSS THE FRANKLIN EXPEDITION, a disaster I'd never heard of. Its vivid images of dead sailors frozen in icy graves stuck with me until I started thinking about this book. Many Americans don't know about the explorers whose boats froze in the Arctic and what happened to them. In Canada, however, people have followed research on the Franklin expedition for years.

Sir John Franklin

For this book especially, I needed to find the "bones" of the story. Read on ...

THIS IS A STORY THAT COULD HAVE DIFFERENT BEGINNINGS.

FIRST:

An expedition set sail from England in 1845. In command was Sir John Franklin, an esteemed captain who had made three voyages of exploration in the name of Queen Victoria. She ruled the British Empire, which held colonies on every continent including Canada. Franklin stood at the helm of Her Majesty's ship *Erebus*, together with her sister ship *HMS Terror*.

The English hoped that Franklin and his men would discover the elusive "Northwest Passage." To succeed, they would have to navigate Canada's icy waters from the Atlantic across the Arctic to the Pacific Ocean. These strange cold lands and waterways had been only partly mapped.

Franklin and the one hundred twenty-eight sailors who served under him sailed into the Wellington Channel amid Canada's Arctic islands and were never heard from again. The British embarked on a quest to find them but stopped the search in 1850. Until very recently, the search remained "at sea."

OR THE STORY COULD GO LIKE THIS:

OR THE STORY COULD GO LIKE THIS:

Back in the 1960s, a little boy sat at the knee of his great-grandmother in their home on King William Island in Nunavut (NOO-nah-voot), then a territory and now a province of Canada. The boy's name was Louie Kamookak. The old woman, Hummahuk, shared many tales with her family. They were Inuit (IN-yew-it) people who lived in the far northern reaches of North America. English explorers first made contact with them in 1576.

Among her stories was one that Louie never forgot. Hummahuk spoke of her own childhood long years before, when she and her father were out walking across King William Island. They came up a ridge and found strange objects on the cold ground. Louie later said:

> They were finding stuff that she [his great-grandmother] later realized were muskets, or a rifle; spoons, and forks, ropes and chain . . .

Hummahuk's father took a dining knife and made an ice chisel from it.

Even more strange was a mound, she said, ". . . and at the end of the mound, there was a rock with markings on it. The mound was the length of a human, and because it was the length of a human, they were afraid to go near it."

Great-grandmother Hummahuk later realized this was a grave, very unlike the way that her people treated their dead. Said Louie:

> Going back to her time, the Inuit had never buried their dead under the ground—they just wrapped them in skins, and the animals would come and take the bodies away.
>
> That was the belief, that you died, and you go back into the world.

Hummahuk's story about the man-sized grave stayed with Louie his whole life. There were other Inuit stories of disaster, too—tales of human bones scattered along an icy trail, bones of the Qallunaat (kah-LU-nay-aat), "white men."

Louie Kamookak grew up to become an amateur historian. Though he left school after ninth grade, he began collecting Inuit stories as a young man. These accounts had been passed down from one generation to the next, an "oral tradition" of keeping history alive. Over time Louie came to think that Hummahuk had seen evidence of the Franklin expedition. He compared her stories with the written records.

In the end Louie Kamookak's work contributed to remarkable discoveries. After more than one hundred seventy years, much of the lost expedition would be found.

A WRITTEN RECORD AND A TRAIL OF BONES

Either way you start the story, it is about the same man.

John Franklin was only fourteen years old when he went in the Royal Navy in 1800. He saw battles at sea and took part in a three-year scientific voyage to far-off Australia. As he rose through the ranks, Franklin achieved the sought-after role of captain on the *Trent*, a whaling ship among others that sailed under the command of David Buchan in 1818 that tried—and failed—to find a northern route between the Atlantic and Pacific oceans, without, of course, being stopped by ice.

In 1825 Franklin made a second voyage to Canada, this time by land from the mouth of the Mackenzie River in toward modern-day Alaska. His goal was to assist in mapping the northern coast, two thousand kilometers of land. Such a success raised him in the navy, and Franklin was knighted with the title "Sir John" in 1829.

And yet . . . there were still five hundred kilometers of unmapped coast. Could this uncharted area, between Barrow Strait and the mainland, be the link to finding the Northwest Passage? In 1845 Franklin, with one hundred twenty-eight officers and crew under his command, left home to find out.

When HMS *Erebus* and *Terror* departed England for Canada, no one expected to see or hear from its crewmen for a year or two. The written record shows that a whaler (whale-hunting ship) spotted the sister ships two months later on July 26, 1845, in Baffin Bay, west of Greenland. That report was the last "official" sighting of the Franklin expedition. (Except for the Inuit, of course.)

Since then the disappearance of Franklin and his men has mystified scores of archaeologists, historians, and scientists.

From what we know, the expedition spent its first winter off Beechey Island in the Wellington Channel. The next summer in 1846, *Erebus* and *Terror* turned south to make their way into Victoria Strait, west of King William Island. Ill fortune met both ships. We now know that on September 12, 1846, they became stuck, *frozen stiff* in pack ice.

With no word from Franklin, England sent three expeditions to search for him. The British Admiralty helped pay for their efforts, as did Franklin's desperate wife, Lady Jane

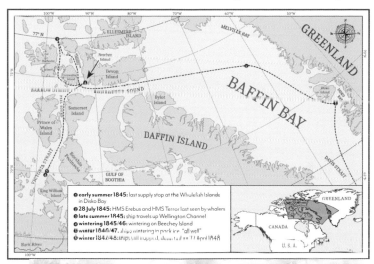

The Franklin Expedition sailed through a waterway in the Arctic Ocean until the ships froze in ice just northwest of King William Island.

Franklin. One search party came via the Pacific Ocean in the west, another traced Franklin's supposed route from the Atlantic into the Northwest Passage, and a third came overland from the Mackenzie River.

Then a chance encounter added to the mystery. Another group from England was sent to make a survey of the west shore of the Boothia Peninsula, which happens to be the most northern point of mainland North America. These mapmakers met some Inuit who had relics from the Franklin expedition and heard their chilling stories. Their leader, a Scottish doctor named John Rae, wrote to the Admiralty in 1854.

> REPULSE BAY, JULY 29
>
> Sir,—I have the honor to mention, for the information of my Lords Commissioners of the Admiralty, that during my journey over the ice and snow this spring, with the view of completing the survey of the west shore of Boothia, I met with Esquimaux [indigenous people] in Pelly Bay, from one of whom I learned that a party of white men (Kablounans) had perished from want of food . . .

Rae learned more details and also bought goods from the Inuit that had belonged to the Franklin expedition, "which places the fate of a portion, if not of all of the then survivors of Sir John Franklin's long-lost party, beyond a doubt—a fate as terrible as the imagination can conceive."

Through a translator, the Inuit man, Innookpoozhejook, told Rae that in the spring of 1850,

> . . . a party of "white men," amounting to about forty, were seen travelling southward over the ice, and dragging a boat with them, by some Esquimaux who were killing seals near the north shore of King William's Land, which is a large island. None of the party could speak the Esquimaux language intelligibly, but by signs the party were made to understand that their ship, or ships, had been crushed by ice, and that they were now going to where they expected to find deer to shoot. From the appearance of the men, all of whom, except one officer, looked thin, they were then supposed to be getting short of provisions, and purchased a small seal from the natives.

There was more, as Innookpoozhejook reported to Rae, bones of dead men everywhere:

> At a later date the same season . . . the bodies of some thirty persons were discovered on the Continent, and five on an island near it . . . Some of the bodies had been buried (probably those of the first victims of famine), some were in a tent or tents, others under the boat, which had been turned over to form a shelter, and several lay scattered about in different directions. Of those found on the island, one was supposed to have been an officer, as he had a telescope

A "Captain May" drew his vision of an ice-bound funeral for someone with the Franklin Expedition.

strapped over his shoulders, and his double-barreled gun lay underneath him.

The Inuit had seen the boney evidence left behind by the starving "flesh eaters." Innookpoozhejook's description of the dead must have chilled Rae to *his* very bones.

From the mutilated state of many of the corpses and the contents of the kettles, it is evident that our wretched countrymen had been driven to the last resource—cannibalism—as a means of prolonging existence.

Cannibalism. Eating the dead. To the high-minded British at home, such an act was . . . Unthinkable! When Rae returned to England, he discovered that his report had hit the newspapers and made *him* a pariah, an outcast. No one wanted to believe his creepy and gruesome stories. Lady Franklin was outraged and held back her promised payment.

ANOTHER GO

In 1857 another Englishman, Francis Leopold McClintock, made another try at finding Franklin—at the request of Lady Jane, who refused to end *her* search even if the Admiralty had. McClintock had already made three fruitless trips, but McClintock had wisely learned how to plan and provision an overland expedition by sledge. (Think of huge sleds with iron runners.) McClintock and his second-in-command, a Lieutenant Hobson, split up their efforts as they cased King William Island. Taking a cue from the Inuit, McClintock traveled by dogsled along the southern coast of the island. McClintock searched the east

In 1859, *Frank Leslie's Illustrated Newspaper* published this illustration depicting the McClintock search party as it discovered the cairn left by members of the Franklin Expedition.

side of King William Island and sent Hobson to search the west side.

Along the way McClintock met Inuit who were living in a "snow village." "I do not think any of them had ever seen white people alive before, but they evidently knew us as friends," he wrote. The Inuit spoke of a shipwreck, a five-day journey on foot to the west coast of King William Island.

McClintock's interpreter spoke with an old woman and a boy thought to be the last to see the shipwreck. Wrote McClintock, "She said many of the white men dropped by the way as they went to the Great River; that some were buried and some were not; they did not themselves witness this, but discovered their bodies during the winter following." Bodies?

Hobson and McClintock both had come across a cairn, a rock pile used to store messages in the wilderness. Inside was a metal tube that protected two notes written on a single piece of paper. The first note, penned by a Lieutenant Gore in 1847, stated that all was well with Franklin and his men. Though locked in ice, the expedition had spent the winter of 1845–1846 with good success. When the ice broke in summer 1846, *Erebus* and *Terror* had sailed to a point five miles (eight kilometers) off the "north extreme of King William's Land." Again Franklin and crew wintered successfully, Gore wrote. The Franklin expedition had survived its first two winters in ice.

But the second note, scrawled around Gore's handwriting by a "Captain Fitzjames" in 1848, changed everything. On

April 22, 1848, Fitzjames wrote, *Terror* and *Erebus* were "deserted" after being frozen in the ice pack since the previous September.

McClintock wrote to the British Admiralty:

> Within a month after Lieutenant Gore placed the record on Point Victory, the much-loved leader of the expedition, Sir John Franklin, was dead; and the following spring found Captain Crozier, upon whom the command had devolved [passed down] at King William's Land, endeavoring to save his starving men, 105 souls in all, from a terrible death by retreating to the Hudson Bay territories up the Back or Great Fish River. A sad tale was never told in fewer words.

No more news from Crozier or his men ever reached England.

McClintock saw that Captain Crozier's men had mounted a lifeboat atop a sledge and dragged it across the ice as they trekked toward the Back River. McClintock estimated that it would take seven men to pull the massive object. Now it stood like a creepy road marker.

And inside the lifeboat? Bones—a pair of skeletons, both missing skulls. One was of a large man, possibly an officer, but it was hard to tell because animals had made a mess of it. The second, found under the boat, was of a smaller man. Had the two died waiting for a rescue? Later three skulls were found at the site, too.

The lifeboat was jammed with a mixed bag of stuff—clothing, combs, toothbrush, sponge, soap, towels, tobacco, silverware and plates, and no food except tea and chocolate. (Oddly, animals hadn't eaten it.) McClintock thought this strange: "a mere accumulation of deadweight of little use, and very likely to break down the strength of the sledge crews."

The search for Franklin continued. Twenty British and American explorers went to the Arctic between 1847 and 1859, plus another eleven missions to resupply those who went first. More followed: all told, as many as thirty-five expeditions.

LISTENING TO THE INUIT

An American from Ohio, Charles Francis Hall, left for the Arctic in 1864 to hunt for Franklin. Hall took time to listen to the indigenous women and men who lived there. He penned two thick books filled with interviews with the Inuit who had met and/or watched the forlorn Franklin men.

Hall noticed that the Inuit, whose name means "people," lived in small groups that didn't interact much. Sometimes groups on one side of an island could barely understand those on the other.

"The language of this people is peculiar to themselves. They have nothing written, and all that they can tell is derived from oral tradition, handed down from parent to child for many generations." *Many* generations, indeed.

Hall met a one-hundred-year-old Inuit woman who spoke of Martin Frobisher, the very first English explorer to make contact with her people two hundred years earlier!

To Hall's good fortune, an Inuit woman named Tookoolito, whom he called "Hannah," could translate the Inuit's words into English. On July 2, 1869, she sat with Hall as he spoke with Innookpoozhejook. He, four other Inuit men, and their families had gone "to search after such things as they could find that belonged to the white men that had died on King William's land."

Charles Francis Hall pictured with two Inuit. There is no record of their names.

Question: What particular time of the year was it?

Answer: Thinks the time of the year about when we returned to this bay encampment,—June 20. Water had begun to make on the ice, and water is a little later making there than here. Snow and ice were inside the boats, and all around.

Question: Did the boats look as if anybody had visited them within two or three years?

Answer: Somebody had been to one of them, for everything was gone out of it.

In the 1930s, a search party came upon human bones thought to belong to the Franklin Expedition.

Question: What did you find in the other boat—the one that the white men [McClintock's earlier party] . . . did not find?

Innookpoozhejook's answer began with common objects.

Answer: Six paddles; many table knives, white handle; one watch; a spyglass that his son has, . . . something like my compass, but no glass about it; tobacco that had been wet and was in flakes or thin pieces; very many tin dishes . . .

Then the Inuit's list turned to flesh and bones.

. . . one whole skeleton with clothes on,– the flesh all on, but dried; many skeleton bones; three skulls. Alongside of the boat a big pile of skeleton bones that had been broken up for the marrow in them; they were near a fireplace; skulls among these. The number of them *ama-su-ad-loo* (a great many)– cannot tell how many. It is certain that some of the men lived on human flesh, for alongside of the boat were some large boots with cooked human flesh in them.

Hannah went on to tell Hall that, after talking with Innookpoozhejook and the other Inuits, that cooking of the bones of the dead took place after Captain Crozier and his men had left to find the Back River.

The Inuit told the horrible truth. Kettles of bones and boots filled with flesh spoke to the desperate hunger of the white men left behind.

Crozier's hopes to reach safety failed. "All 105 men who set out for the Back River perished, and reconstructions of events that led to that result have largely been based on discoveries of their bodies, bones, and graves," wrote Dr. Douglas Stenton, a Canadian archaeologist who worked for the Government of Nunavut Department of Culture and Heritage.

Hall hoped to learn more about the fate of Franklin's men maybe to rescue a few.

The site of the "Boat Place" burial, as Stenton called it. A hint of a skull appeared in the ground (*left*), and it and other bones were soon unearthed (*right*).

Dr. Douglas Stenton excavating the
"Boat Place" burial

Although he did find the skeleton of one of Franklin's officers, Hall's search for the possible survivors failed, and he returned to the United States.

🏠 🏠 🏠

And in the meantime, the Inuit stories of ice-bound ships, heaps of bones, and their meeting with starving white men all filtered down through their families.

Louie Kamookak yearned to find Sir John Franklin's grave and see the explorer's remains returned home to England. In fact, he had found a set of large flat stones, possible sign of a burial, in winter 2004. Kamookak had marked it so that he could return for a better look the next summer.

But Louie's own life took a different turn. His health declined. In 2016 he returned to King Edward Island to look for Franklin once more, but warmer temperatures and rain had turned the icy tundra to mud. Franklin's grave stayed hidden.

Louie Kamookak died in April 2018.

Louie Kamookak cleaning
Arctic char, a fish

FACTLET

❦

ESKIMOS? GETTING THE
WORDS RIGHT

THE INUIT AND OTHER people who lived in the far reaches of North America, Greenland, and eastern Russia were called "Eskimos" by outsiders.

Yet this term is not what these indigenous people call themselves. Nor do we now. In Canada and Greenland *Inuit* is the best term. *Inuit* means "people." In Alaska, where indigenous people descended from different groups, there are Aleuts, Athabaskans, Inupiaq, and Yupik, among others. To many, the term *Eskimo* isn't correct.

The Oxford English Dictionary is my go-to for terminology, how we use words to express our ideas. Here's the top definition of the term *Eskimo*.

A member of any of several closely related indigenous peoples inhabiting the Arctic coasts of Canada and Greenland, and parts of Alaska and the Russian Far East.

In Canada and Greenland, and more generally, the word *Inuit* (Inuit n.) has superseded the word *Eskimo*, which has come to be regarded as offensive (partly through the associations of the now discredited etymology "one who eats raw flesh"). *Eskimo*, however, is the only term which applies to the Eskimo peoples as a whole, including not only the Inuit of Canada, Greenland, and Alaska, but also the Yupik of Siberia and the Inupiaq of Alaska. *Eskimo* is still widely used, especially in Alaska and in anthropological, archaeological, and linguistic contexts.

For general writing and speaking, the word *Eskimo* has gone out of fashion. It's best to ask indigenous people—Native Americans in the United States and Aboriginal people in Canada—how they like to call themselves.

CHAPTER FOUR

THE CALAMITY OF JANE

WE BEGIN WITH A STORY ABOUT WHAT IS CALLED "THE Starving Time," in the earliest days of America. About what people can do if they get *really hungry*. If you have a delicate stomach—or you're eating a snack right now—you might not want to read any further.

In the summer of 1609, an English ship sailed up the James River in colonial Virginia and dropped anchor off a small peninsula. A fort had stood there for two years. Like the river, the fort was named for King James I of England. When the newcomers arrived, Jamestown Fort grew its numbers to two hundred fourteen, mostly men and a few women and children.

An artistic rendering of the Jamestown Colony prepared by the U.S. National Park Service

By the next spring, only sixty would still be alive.

The Jamestown Fort was a miserable place that summer. Two years into their big plan to establish a colony, its few people had little to show for all their dreams of riches and wealth. Two-thirds of the first settlers died in the first nine months, and, for the most part, their bones went into graves. But more hopefuls kept coming, making long voyages on stinking ships to get there, all in the name of the Virginia Company, a firm appointed by the king to colonize the "new world."

Many settlers were gentleman business types in search of gold and jewels to send home to England. They knew next to nothing about farming or working with their hands. The first settlers had planted their fort in a mosquito-ridden, saltwater marsh. It turned out that Jamestown was a horrible place for growing anything. So when more newcomers landed that August of 1609, there was little to feed them, no crops to harvest, and nothing put aside for the winter.

What was more, the settlers had turned once-friendly indigenous people against them. The Powhatans, who lived along the Virginia coast, grew crops of corn, squash, and beans. They had shown the newcomers how to grow them, too. But hospitality turned to hostility. When their capable leader John Smith hurt himself, he went back to England. (This was the same John Smith supposedly saved from execution by the Powhatan Pocahontas.) Now the Powhatans decided they'd had enough of the colonists. They surrounded the fort, killed those who ventured out, and bided their time.

So in 1609 the Englishmen began to starve.

The colonists first slaughtered their horses and ate them. As things went to the dogs they ate them, too, and cats and rats and snakes and roots of plants they couldn't name. Then they took to boiling pieces of leather, which didn't satisfy anyone.

And so they began gnawing at the bones of each other. A survivor wrote later, "famine beginning to look ghastly and pale in every face, that nothing was spared to maintain life and to do those things which seem incredible . . ." Like dogs, the settlers licked up the blood flowing from their sick neighbors.

It was said they ate the dead, whom they dug out of graves and butchered like hogs. One crazed man killed his wife, seasoned her, and ate all but her head. He was tortured and burned at the stake.

John Smith later made a snarky remark about the murdered woman: "Now whether she was better roasted, boyled [boiled] or carbonado'd [barbecued], I know not, but of such a dish as powdered wife."

Smith didn't mean the wife wore makeup. "Powdered" meant *salted*.

Thus went the story of cannibalism on American soil, as written by the survivors at Jamestown. Then came the cover-up. The sixty survivors of the Starving Times were actually on board a rescue boat, setting sail for home, when a giant English ship arrived with food and supplies and yet more settlers for Jamestown. A new boss replaced the old ones who had made such a mess of things, and he ordered the fort to be knocked down, covered up, and rebuilt. The settlers went on to make a success of their venture by growing tobacco and sending it off to fill the pipes of Englishmen. Soon there was little left to remind anyone of the Starving Time.

Except the written word. Those gentlemen who returned to England took up their pens, parchment, and ink. They wrote such graphic, lurid descriptions of the cannibalism at Jamestown that later historians couldn't believe their eyes when they read them.

Eventually Williamsburg replaced Jamestown as Virginia's capital. Jamestown fell into ruin and was mostly forgotten until archaeologists began digging around the island (a peninsula earlier) in 1993. Led by William Kelso, the archaeologists uncovered many skeletons as they worked in the old settlement. Many still wore their clothes instead of shrouds, a sign of hurried burials AND possibly due to disease. In those days clothes were awfully expensive, and few folks were buried in them rather than pass them on.

It didn't make sense that so many had died, even when scholars discovered that a terrible drought had hit Jamestown during 1609. Some guessed that the wells at Jamestown were poisoned by arsenic and/or the settler's own excrement.

But the researchers found no sign that cannibalism had any place in Virginia's earliest years. Perhaps, they thought, the man-eating stories were made up by the survivors to defend their lousy job of running a colony.

Dead men tell no tales, eaten or not.

Then on a Friday afternoon in April 2012, a student working in a long-buried cellar found a few teeth. Human teeth. She showed her discovery to the archaeologist in charge, but it was getting late. They covered the teeth back up. Even archaeologists take weekends off.

On Monday they returned to the teeth and more: half a human cranium, bits of bone, and the very top part of a leg bone, a right tibia. From all appearances, the skull had been chopped in two. The other half was missing. The archaeologists wondered what was in their hands. All the other

These few bones are what was found of "Jane," the fourteen-year-old victim of the Starving Times.

bones in that ancient trash pile were from animals. Why then would these few human remains lie there with the dogs and horses and squirrels?

The archaeologists knew that the old cellar had once served as a kitchen. The building above it had collapsed and left a hole. Sometime in 1610 the cellar became a dump where people went to stash their trash.

There's nothing like a garbage pit for finding hidden gems. In that old cellar the archaeologists found forty-seven thousand artefacts. That's forty-seen thousand individual pieces of evidence hinting at the lives of these mysterious settlers. Stuff like pottery shards, bits of armor and military equipment, trade beads, seashells, and of course all those bones.

But why the half a human skull, those teeth, and the tibia? The diggers treated the site like a crime scene—they didn't think they were dealing with a common grave. They turned to an expert at the Smithsonian Institution. Dr. Doug Owsley, a forensic anthropologist, had examined thousands of ancient skeletons. He worked at modern crime scenes, too, helping police detectives by studying the victims' bones.

In the lab at Jamestown, the conservators cleaned away four hundred years of damp brown soil that held the mysterious bones. They took great care not to mark them with their tiny picks and brushes, because the surfaces of those bones might tell them something. As the surfaces of the cranium were cleaned, chop marks appeared on both the forehead and in back.

But how old was this person? Luckily, the researchers had a mandible (a jaw bone), and it spoke volumes. An x-ray clearly showed a third molar, aka "wisdom tooth," growing inside the bone. It was good-sized and starting to form a root.

Any wise forensic scientist knows that wisdom teeth don't erupt from the jaw until the late teen years. (Lots of high school kids can tell you it's a painful experience.) Hence, the research team figured that the mandible came from a young person, about age fourteen.

That conclusion matched another hint on the cranium. The plates of bone that form the crania of babies and young kids don't fuse until the teen years. Open sutures, which look like inky squiggles across the surface of the cranium, showed that the various parts of the skull hadn't fully grown together.

They knew they had a young person, but was it boy or girl? The cranium offered clues about that matter, as well. Rub your forehead. If it's smooth and generally vertical (straight up and down), you're likely a girl. Boys' foreheads, on the other hand, are prone to sloping back a bit and have a heavier ridge above the eyebrows.

There's more. Behind the ear canals are bony protrusions called the mastoid processes, the spot where neck muscles attach to the bone. At the base of the cranium is another bony ridge where other neck muscles attach in back. In guys, whose necks tend to be bigger than girls', these bony out-croppings are larger, to handle larger muscles.

The mystery cranium, with its vertical forehead, small mastoid process, and smooth neck ridge, showed every sign that the researchers were working with a girl. They named her Jane, the classic tag for an unidentified female, as in "Jane Doe." As it happened, Jane was a popular name for girls when she walked the earth, as well.

But was she English? Again the experts turned to the bones for answers. First of all, Jane's cranium was the size and shape of other people who lived in England at that time. (There's a whole collection of crania in Cambridge, England, for anthropologists to study.)

Second, the researchers tested small samples of her bone, hunting for isotopes of oxygen, carbon, and nitrogen. Over time food leaves chemical traces of these elements in our bones and teeth. Jane's bones showed signs that she ate wheat and barley in England—which left one kind of carbon isotope. A different isotope proved that in Virginia she ate corn, the New World variety that grows on a cob.*

*To become totally confused, try asking someone British for a piece of corn. You'll be handed a sheaf of wheat. In British English, wheat is "corn." Corn (on the cob) is "maize." Indigenous Americans first grew it and introduced it to Europeans. Amazing, huh?

These chemical clues showed that Jane probably hailed from somewhere along the coastal plains of southern England, farm country. She had been well-fed, an indicator she might be a child in a middle- or upper-crust family. Or she could have been a maidservant lucky enough to eat her master's and mistress's leftovers.

But the research had far to go. Those suspect marks on the front and back of Jane's cranium—what were *they* about?

The researchers hauled out their biggest magnifiers and took a look. Jane's mandible showed a series of very thin cuts, cuts so fine they wouldn't have shown up otherwise. The cuts seemed to have been made in a sawing motion, with a sharp knife. Knife strokes along the bottom of Jane's jaw looked as though someone had tried to deflesh it, like you'd scrape the kernels off a corn cob. The researchers compared this knife job to animal bones, and they concluded that Jane's butcher was an amateur. For whatever reason, either inexperience or outright disgust at cutting up a dead girl, the person with the knife hadn't wielded it with the same confidence as a butcher.

Jane's cranium had chop marks all over—in the middle of her forehead, under her right eye socket, and on the back of her skull—plus a single puncture through her left temporal bone. Dr. Owsley, who had studied some ten thousand skeletons doing his job, spelled out what happened to Jane.

First of all, she wasn't murdered. Fourteen-year-old Jane was one of the unlucky ones who starved to death that winter of 1609–1610. Jane may have starved, but others were ready to do what they must to stay alive, and they butchered her remains. Eating animal brains, tongues, and cheeks was perfectly acceptable at the time, as some do now. Knowing that brain tissue deteriorates very fast, they went for Jane's head first.

Dr. Douglas Owsley explained.

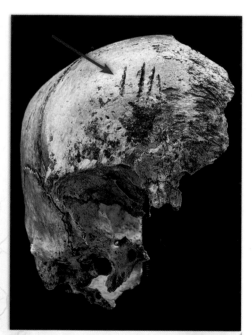

Strike marks line up along the top of "Jane's" forehead.

> The chops to the forehead are very tentative, very incomplete . . . Then, the body was turned over, and there were four strikes to the back of the head, one of which was the strongest and split the skull in half. A penetrating wound was then made to the left temple, probably by a single-sided knife, which was used to pry open the head and remove the brain.

Other knife blows beneath the right eye socket also show signs that her cheeks were defleshed.

When the experts moved on to Jane's tibia, they learned more. It had been chopped from behind in order to break the shaft and expose the marrow in the long bone. This time the blows looked like a professional had made them. The conclusion: More than one cannibal took a knife to Jane. Like meat in a butcher shop, she was dismembered and scattered among those who ate her. Only those few bones of this young woman were recovered from that cellar kitchen in the Jamestown fort.

Working with half a cranium, a jawbone, and a few bits of bone, the Smithsonian folks gave Jane a computer-generated head and turned her into a model citizen. Their 3D model sported the features of a typical girl born in southern England in Jane's day—light brown hair, blue eyes, and fair skin. Assuming that she wore her hair up in a bun, the experts also added a coif, a sort of stringless bonnet to cover her hair, as any proper young woman would in 1609.

A facial reconstruction of "Jane"

Where's the rest of Jane? No sign of her has turned up anywhere else, but it's possible that more of her bones and other bits and pieces of women and men await discovery near the old fort. In 2013 the partial skeletons of four Jamestown men came to light during a dig in the old Jamestown church. The four men had died in 1608, 1609, and 1610, about the same time as Jane died. Unlike poor Jane, they had been buried near the altar of the Jamestown church, which marked their status as VIPs.

A MODERN-DAY MOUNTAINTOP SURVIVAL

About three hundred fifty years after that bleak winter in Jamestown Colony, another disaster took place. The tragedy—and its story of survival—unfolded in the high Andes in South America. On Friday, October 13, 1972, a plane from Uruguay crashed into the side of a mountain. It was carrying forty-two passengers, many of them members, family, and fans of an Uruguayan rugby team.

Twenty-seven of its passengers died on impact. At fourteen thousand feet (four thousand two hundred seventy meters) above sea level, in the frozen and snowy cold, the survivors were stranded. At night everyone packed into the fuselage to stay warm in the face of below-zero temperatures. They tuned in to a tiny transistor radio and heard that the authorities had stopped searching for them. The group was on their own, with no food and only a little wood from packing crates to burn.

One of the rugby team's bolder members had offered a plan to solve their hunger. Lack of food was already taking its toll on their brains and bodies as they began the horrendous process of starvation. Forty years later, rugby player Roberto Canessa explained his ideas:

> Our story became world famous because of how we survived: by eating those who had died. It was, by far, our most eccentric idea, one that was simultaneously simple and audacious, and perhaps inconceivable. But we had felt the sensation of our bodies consuming themselves just to remain alive, the feeling of total and complete starvation, where merely standing up was enough to make us dizzy and pass out from hunger. We experienced that primal primitive instinct of true hunger—and perhaps that's what wild animals feel. It's something innate, irrational.

The survivors set up camp as best they could. They made exploratory hikes to scavenge stuff from the crash site, which stretched a long distance They also scouted for possible routes that might lead them through the mountains to find help.

It was after one of these forlorn hikes that Fernando "Nando" Parrado, another player, wrapped his head around their situation:

> The days I'd spent away from the Fairchild had given me perspective, and now I saw with fresh eyes the gruesomeness that had become a normal part of our daily lives. There were piles of bones scattered outside the fuselage. Large body parts—someone's forearm, a human leg from hip to toes—were stored near the opening of the fuselage for easy access . . . And for the first time I saw human skulls in the bone pile. When we first started eating human flesh, we consumed mostly small pieces of meat cut from the large muscles. But as time passed and the food supply diminished, we had no choice but to broaden our diet. For some time, we had

been eating livers, kidneys, and hearts, but meat was in such short supply now that we would have to split skulls to get at the brains inside . . . To the ordinary mind, these actions may seem incomprehensibly repulsive, but the instinct to survive runs very deep, and when death is so near, a human being gets used to anything.

From the beginning of their ordeal, the group knew that two or three of them would have to hike out of the crash site and go for help. The assignment fell to Canessa and Parrado. On December 12 they began their trek over the mountains. Over icy days and nights so cold their toes turned black, Canessa and Parrado hiked. When they descended, signs of warmer soil and small, red, biting bugs held promise.

Roberto Canessa (*standing left*) as medical workers treat Nando Parrado at the crash site

On Day 7 they noticed that the late afternoon sunlight hung on longer than usual. It was the sign of a break in the mountains, a pass and a path to civilization. On December 20, Day 9, they made contact with a man on horseback.

Canessa and Parrado had to face their own consciences and then to tell the world exactly

Dirt is sprinkled on the mass grave of those left on the mountain.

how they had stayed alive for seventy-two days. They begged for forgiveness, first from their own families. Then came time to ask their dead friends' families to forgive them for their heinous act.

There was general agreement that the dead should remain on the mountain. They were buried in a mass grave, some already skeletons but others still frozen. The only exception were the remains of one young man who had studied dairy farming. Before he died, he asked for a message to be passed on to his father. He did not want to be left behind on the mountain.

His wishes were honored.

FACTLET

FACTS ON FLESH AND BONE EATERS

1. Cannibalism has been practiced by people on every continent since prehistoric times.

2. About the time that Jane came to Virginia, the English and other Europeans happily drank human blood and ate powdered bones, hoping for a cure from seizures, back problems, arthritis, warts, and zits. Ground-up human skull mixed with chocolate was a favored recipe to treat people with bleeding on the brain. King Charles II of England made his own medicine with ground skull and alcohol known as the "King's Drops."

3. A generation of moviegoers will forever remember Hannibal the Cannibal, the liver-eating psychiatrist portrayed in the 1991 film *Silence of the Lambs*, as one of the scariest villains ever.

CHAPTER FIVE

BENJAMIN FRANKLIN'S BASEMENT BONEYARD

36 Craven Street, London—the only existing home of Ben Franklin

IT LOOKS LIKE ALL THE OTHER buildings along Craven Street, a row of stylish homes in London, England, at the center of the action in the British Empire in the late 1700s. The house at 36 Craven Street, however, is special to Americans. From 1757 until 1774, the lodging was home to Benjamin Franklin, a founding father of the United States.

More than two hun-
dred years after, his
London admirers decided
that Franklin's old house
should become a museum.
Renovations began in
1998. But when a construction worker dug into the
basement floor, a call went
out to the Metropolitan
Police.

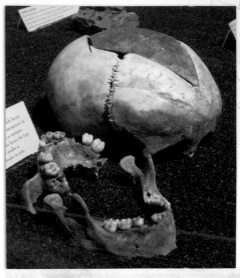

This skull had been used for study at
36 Craven Street.

The workman had dug
into a pit. Of bones. Lots
of bones and likely from a number of people. The policeman
had never seen anything like it—and he had been on the
force for thirty years. Was this a crime scene? He called the
coroner to investigate the dank, stony pit.

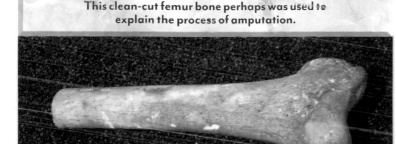

This clean-cut femur bone perhaps was used to
explain the process of amputation.

The coroner, a physician himself, inspected the bones. Later he went on camera to explain their odd features.

Here for example is a femur but the curious thing here it's been cut across. Why is that, that is not usual? Similarly here is a skull and the skull has been cut across there, I mean absolutely sawn . . . so it is perfectly clear that these have been interfered with.

The coroner called an archaeologist, Simon Hillson of University College London, to date the bones. The adult's skull hinted at the use of a straight saw. The kind of a saw that a surgeon in Franklin's time might have had in his medical bag. Hillson, who studies the biology and history of human remains, noted that some others bore saw cuts, too.

Professor Hillson decided that the saw cuts were "postmortem," after death, because they had not healed. The skeletal remains of a newborn baby also lay in the pit. The tiny bones were "an even more unsettling find" to the researchers who studied them.

The pit as well held bird and animal bones, among them the skeleton of a green sea turtle. (Green sea turtles are large and can grow up to five feet [one and one-half meters] long.) Amid its bones were tiny balls of liquid mercury—the kind you'd find in your grandmother's old thermometer—and toxic to boot.

But what did these have to do with Benjamin Franklin? Was he a killer hiding behind a mask of respectability and charm? *Here* was a mystery, mixing history AND archaeology.

Benjamin Franklin, 1757, by David Martin

🏛 🏛 🏛

When Franklin arrived in London in 1757, he took up residence at 36 Craven Street, a lodging house and the home of a widow named Margaret Stevenson and her daughter, Polly. (Franklin's wife, Deborah, had stayed at home in Philadelphia; she was afraid to sail to England.)

Margaret, Polly, and Ben became fast friends, and Ben treated Polly like a daughter. When Polly fell in love and married a doctor who also had rooms at 36 Craven Street, it was Ben who walked her down the aisle.

Young Dr. William Hewson had the keen mind and curiosity that Benjamin Franklin admired. Hewson focused on the circulatory and lymphatic systems in humans, how blood circulated and how the body fights infection.

He studied animal corpses to learn more about the subject. At the Royal Society in London, the eminent group of scholars and thinkers, Hewson lectured on the anatomy

William Hewson, date unknown

of . . . a green sea turtle. 🦴 He injected mercury into the dead creature to show how liquid flowed through its vessels, to show its *anatomy*—how it was built— AND its *physiology*—how it worked.

The green sea turtle talk impressed other scientists. Franklin helped pave the way for Hewson to gain entry into the Royal Society. Franklin was a Fellow of the Royal Society, thanks to his study of electricity. (Do you remember that famous story about Franklin's experiment with a kite and a key in a thunderstorm?)

Diplomat by day, Benjamin Franklin was a scientist at night. Uncommonly gifted, he also was a philosopher, and he asked deep questions about life and God. Franklin was a follower of the Enlightenment, when scholars—men and (often ignored) women—used critical thinking to study the natural world and the skies above.

William Hewson had the same mindset, though he focused on a quiet pursuit. Dr. Hewson was an anatomist. He attached a small outbuilding to the back of his house, where he invited medical students to do hands-on research of the human body.

Certainly, say today's scholars, Benjamin Franklin knew all about it—how else to explain the disgusting smells of rotting bodies coming from the back of the house at 36 Craven Street? It was a crowded neighborhood, where people did their business in chamber pots and privies. In William Hewson's anatomy laboratory, the act of examining corpses and bottling up specimens would have had a special and horrid odor.

But to study anatomy, one needed a cadaver. So where did Hewson find them?

Shhh . . . It might have been days of the Enlightenment, but not all believed the human body should be cut up and analyzed. In England the only legal supply of cadavers were bodies of executed criminals. There were plenty of those, but demand exceeded supply.

Teacher-researchers like Hewson turned to grave robbers for cadavers. *Resurrection men* was the wry term for these seedy robbers who "resurrected" bodies from graves and sold them for hard cash. Over time grave robbing had become an art form carried out under the cover of night. A talented resurrection man easily slipped into an unguarded cemetery, broke into a grave, and bagged a body with little evidence left behind. Risky and difficult most times, but it paid well.

But what happened once a cadaver had been completely picked apart to bones? How did Hewson and his fellow anatomists dispose of their research samples? At 36 Craven Street, Dr. Hewson neatly buried the bones in a square pit one meter wide and one meter long—roughly three feet by three feet. In the very pit that two hundred years later they were discovered by accident.

In a strange twist of fate, William Hewson died doing what he loved. He cut himself during a dissection, and deadly bacteria entered his bloodstream. Dr. Hewson, now known as the "father of hematology"—the study of blood— died of *septicemia*, blood poisoning. He was only thirty-five years old.

Benjamin Franklin left England in 1774, ready to return home to Philadelphia. He would see America win independence from Great Britain and create our democracy by helping to write the Constitution of the United States in 1789.

CADAVERS—NECESSARY, NEEDED, ABUSED

Cadavers. Human beings, once, who now serve as objects of study in medical schools. Cadaver dissection, from skin to bones and head to toe, is not the most pleasant of topics. But cadavers are vital for first-year medical students to study anatomy. Which is exactly what a Harvard med student had written to his friend back in 1775. Neal Rubinstein, associate professor at Perelman School of Medicine, said, "Most physicians don't cut into a body when they're practicing medicine, but they have to know what's underneath if they stick a needle here or there. Almost every physician needs to have a good three-dimensional picture of the body in their head."

Once upon a time in human history, doctors were expected to fix people's aches and pains *without* knowing anatomy. What was more, they were forbidden to study a person's insides, because human dissection was illegal.

Early histories of medicine tell us that two Greek physicians dissected cadavers of condemned criminals about 250 BCE. Even the Greeks, praised for their ways of learning about the world, didn't take deep dives into learning anatomy. When the Roman Catholic Church ruled life in Europe during the Middle Ages, monks and nuns cared for the sick in hospitals, and doctors worked to solve suffering and pain. But the Church outlawed human dissection even if it could teach doctors new things. There were grave consequences for curious anatomists.

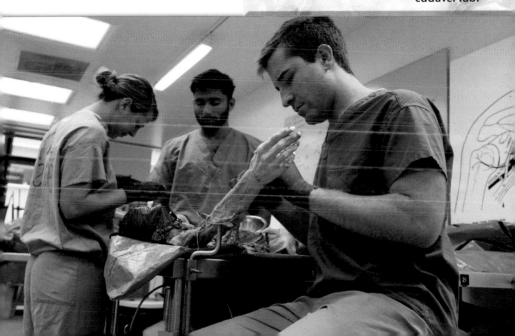

Medical students at work in a modern-day cadaver lab.

During the Middle Ages important people who died in far-off lands were cooked and defleshed so their bones could be sent home and buried in the local graveyard or crypt. Without refrigeration, the bodies wouldn't have lasted through the long journey.

Especially among dignitaries dying far from home, it was customary to disembowel the cadaver, dismember and cook it so that the bones were dissevered from the flesh. The bones could then be easily transported and interred. This practice was known as "embalming more teutonico," an originally German custom that became widespread by the thirteenth century.

Teutonico, or *Teutonic* in English, refers to something German.

Because they died far from home, the bodies of Saint Louis XI of France, who died in 1270, and Saint Thomas Aquinas, who died in 1274, each received this treatment for transport. It came, however, to be vehemently opposed by the papacy. Pope Boniface XIII stopped the practice cold in 1299.

The strongest possible expressions were used to condemn the custom of chopping up

> and boiling the body in water: it was called
> a "savage abuse" ... and the custom is called
> "cruel" and "horrendous for the faithful ..."
> This abomination was considered impious
> both in the eyes of the Divine Majesty as in
> those of humans, and the body thus treated
> would be denied Christian burial.

Times change. The Middle Ages gave way to the Renaissance, the "rebirth" of the ways of the old Greeks and Romans long before. Dissection slowly came into favor, especially in Italy. A popular medical school in Bologna got permission to conduct the first "official" public dissection of executed criminals. The event looked more like a three-man performance than scientific investigation.

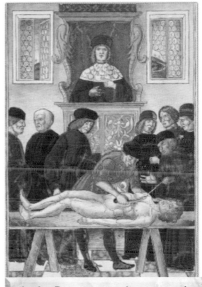

The cast of players included the Lector (the presenter, who was an anatomist), the Ostensor (the pointer), and the Sector (the cutter). As the Lector read from a written text, the Ostensor pointed to a target area on the cadaver, and right there, the Sector cut into the body. How

In this Renaissance dissection, the Lector stands above on the rostrum as the Ostensor points to the body, directing the Sector where to cut. This image appeared as a woodcut illustration in *Fasciculus medicinae*, published in 1491.

odd for the "anatomist" to not take a single look into the cadaver *at all* during this display!

The least of these was the man who did the cutting, most likely a barber-surgeon. For hundreds of years these cutters of hair and shavers of beards did modest medical procedures. Barber-surgeons were at work way up to the 1700s when Benjamin Franklin needed his locks trimmed. Look at the red-and-white-striped poles in barber shops, which hearken back to when barbers did a bit of bloodletting.

As cadaver study grew more popular, so grew the need for cadavers. Society approved dissection on convicted criminals, for one. But demand for the dead was bigger than the supply of corpses, so an underground trade in body snatching became big business.

No wonder that Franklin, the esteemed statesman-scientist, had not written a word about the goings-on in his house. It was illegal . . . no bones about that!

But that bevy of bones in Ben's basement turned out to be one set among many of scattered skeletons among medical schools—not only in London. In Toronto and Montréal, Canada, grave robbers delivered newly buried corpses for students to dissect. Clusters of cast-off cadavers—or their bones, to be exact—were discovered in New York. In Georgia, Maine, Virginia, Michigan, Illinois, Ohio. In New Orleans, Louisiana, two medical schools—across the street from each other—competed for students. One offered "the finest dissecting room in the country."

To have a dissecting room, that school needed cadavers. The grim truth was that most bodies supplied to student doctors were not donations, but bodies either bought—or more likely, stolen. Bodies of poor people, abandoned people, and enslaved people comprised most medical cadavers at the time.

A disturbing case turned up at the Medical College of Georgia in Augusta in summer 1989. The old building was being remodeled, and as workmen made their way into its dirt basement, they found a gruesome surprise. There were bones, ten thousand of them, planted in layers along with pieces of medical tools that dated back one hundred years.

The basement soon became an archaeological site. In time, books and articles shared uneasy news. Most of the bones buried beneath the medical school were of African Americans, most likely snatched from the grave.

The name of one enslaved man, Grandison Harris, has stuck to that story of the Georgia Medical College. Harris was purchased in 1852 by the college's seven teaching doctors in to do a sinister, if necessary, job: to steal newly buried bodies for dissection. Breaking the rules of slaveholding, Harris was taught to read and write. That way he could scan death notices in the newspaper before his nighttime raids in cemeteries.

Harris was a "resurrection man." Harris's graveyard of choice was Augusta's Cedar Grove Cemetery, home mostly to graves of Black people. He followed the pattern that

Grandison Harris (*back row, without cap*)
posed with these graduating doctors at the
Georgia Medical College.

others used: arriving in the dead of night, shifting flowers and memorials from a fresh grave, digging down to the coffin, cracking open the lid, removing the body into a sack, and quickly refilling the grave and rearranging flowers on top so there was no hint of disturbance.

After the Civil War, Harris, no longer enslaved, continued working as a paid employee for the medical college.

When the bones were found in 1989, researchers moved in to unearth the story behind the burials. Anthropologist Robert Blakely of Georgia State University led the investigation. The remains were removed and cataloged. They told a valuable story.

Our whole scientific team has a deep respect for these individuals. The remains of these people, who may not have had a glamorous life are now writing history. We approach each aspect of the study with great sensitivity, because we're talking about real people who are the ancestors of real people who are alive today.

Their remains were reburied in Cedar Grove Cemetery.

Something similar happened in 1994 during renovation at the old Medical College of Virginia in Richmond. Human bodies, now turned to bones, had been stashed in a brick well on the site. Investigators looked back one hundred fifty years and realized that the site had been used for medical research for many years.

The school had employed its own resurrection man named Chris Baker. Baker, likely born enslaved, had procured cadavers either by buying bodies of the poor *or* by robbing them from African American cemeteries. It took a research team at the Smithsonian Institution in Washington, DC, more than fifteen years to sort and identify the bones.

> . . . a minimum of forty-four adults (individuals fifteen years and older) and nine children (ages fourteen years and younger) represented by at least nineteen fairly intact bodies plus partial remains of an additional thirty-four individuals.
>
> Males and females are represented, and African and European ancestries are conveyed in the remains of additional thirty-four individuals.

University and state officials had to sit down and figure out the best way to remember the men, women, and children whose bodies were stolen for medical research. One idea was a memorial on campus. A Black professor pointed out that their descendants should take part in the planning.

🏛 🏛 🏛

Up north, Harvard University also made the newspapers in 1999 when a campus chapel was renovated. As in London and Georgia, bones were discovered in the basement, another medical school legacy. Harvard's student newspaper, the *Crimson*, detailed the university's legacy of cadaver seeking, including the notorious Spunker Club of Harvard medical students who took pride in their

A midnight foray into the Medical Room in Holden Chapel.

Dr. Nathan Hayward drew this cartoon of skullduggery—bad behavior—that took place at Harvard University. It was published around 1850.

quick, clean grave robbing in the 1770s. Among them was John Warren, whose name is legendary at Harvard. In a letter he wrote in 1775, young Mr. Warren insisted that grave robbing wasn't so bad. What was worse was getting caught!

> [This particular grave robbery] was done with so little decency and caution . . . It need scarcely be said that it could not have been the work of any of our friends of the Sp–r [Spunker] Club . . . where the necessities of society are in conflict with the law, and with public opinion, the crime consists . . . not in the deed, but in permitting its discovery.

Obviously, families of these stolen dead were hurt and angry and cried out for action. The Act to Protect the Sepulchers of the Dead in 1815 was supposed to put a stop to body snatching in Massachusetts. Harvard, which had medical students to teach, devised a new plan to locate other bodies. These were sourced in neighboring New York.

John Warren, by the way, went on to become an esteemed professor of anatomy and surgery at Harvard Medical School.

THE SORDID SAGA OF JOHN SCOTT HARRISON

No one was safe from resurrection men! Sometimes, bodies of the well-to-do also were spirited out of their graves and quietly transported to medical schools.

In the heart of America, the *Cincinnati Enquirer* told its readers about an incident west of the city:

During the past few days the citizens of North Bend . . . had been disturbed by rumors of the presence of human ghouls who were in waiting to violate the resting places of their dead, and hurry, in the dead of night, the bodies, their illegitimate prey, off to the secrecy of the dissecting-room or the dead-house of the medical college.

On May 29, 1878, family and friends gathered at the Congress Green Cemetery near the Ohio River to mourn the loss of the Honorable John Scott Harrison. The beloved old man, once a U.S. congressman, had died suddenly, found dead in his bedroom. His open grave lay only steps away from that of his father, President William Henry Harrison.

John Harrison had thirteen children. One of his sons, also named John, was present at the burial service. He wandered over to look at the fresh grave of his friend Augustus Devin. Young Devin—only twenty-three—had died of tuberculosis, the horrific disease that took the lives of young and old.

Devin's grave had been robbed!

The Harrison family made sure that their dead father's grave was dug deeper than most. The casket was placed

John Scott Harrison, date unknown

inside a metal vault and covered with a huge stone for even better protection. For the next month, a guard stood watch over the grave.

John Harrison suspected that Devin's body had been stolen by a resurrection man. The day after his father's funeral, Harrison headed east to Cincinnati, home to several medical colleges. The next day he and a cousin read in the *Cincinnati Enquirer* about a "sensation" at three o'clock early that morning. A buggy had entered an alley near the Ohio Medical College. "It proceeded about halfway [down the alley] when something white was taken out and disappeared... The general impression was that a 'stiff' was being smuggled into the Ohio Medical College."

Harrison went to the police and a search warrant was issued. "The Search Began," the newspaper said, as Harrison and detectives scoured every room, box, barrel, and pile of lumber and stones from cellar to garret, the attic.

In the cellar they found first a huge "chute" or passageway leading from the suspicious gate opening into the alley . . . which connected with an up-and-down shoot or well running from the cellar to the top of the five-story building. These were for the reception of the bodies as delivered by the resurrectionists, and the elevation by windlass [a pulley system] to dissecting rooms above. These and the great furnace in the cellar which is used for the cremation of the flesh after it is cut from the bones of the subjects, were carefully searched, but without finding anything. Upstairs they searched through the various rooms finding nothing until they came to a dissecting-room

Here was a student at work vigorously upon a "subject." He was dressed in coarse overalls and shirt to protect his clothing from the blood and offal of the putrefying body . . .

What Harrison and the others saw next disturbed them even more. They laid eyes on whole bodies and body parts of once-living people of all ages and races, now scattered about on dissection tables.

The medical school janitor who led them through the place acted shadily, and a sharp-eyed policeman deduced that this employee was hiding something in a top-floor room. The search party tracked upstairs to find it jammed with boxes, bundles, papers, rubbish, and bones. In a far corner near a window, a windlass and rope ran down through a hole in the floor.

Detective Thomas Snelbaker tugged at the rope. "It was taut . . . 'Here is somebody,' he said, and seizing the crank began to turn the windlass."With each turn, a body rose up the chute. Now level with the floor, the

"The Injecting Room and Windlass" published in the *Cincinnati Enquirer*, May 31, 1878. Harrison's body was discovered here.

dead man hung naked, robbed of his grave clothes except for a tattered shirt covering the head.

"It is not the man,"John Harrison said firmly. His friend Augustus Devin had wasted away from tuberculosis. Clearly, this man was not skin and bones as Devin had been.

But the detective asked Harrison to look at the dead man's face. They hoisted the body from the chute and laid it on the floor. Incisions in the neck to release the blood indicated that it was being prepped as a cadaver. Harrison gently raised the covering from the face. It was an old man, his white beard chopped squarely off and white hair close-cropped in back. Solemn and quiet, John Harrison bent down to take a parting look at the dead face.

Then his own face went white and he nearly fell into the others' arms.

Still Mr. Harrison was silent, his blanched
face still growing paler, as with eyes starting
from the sockets he gazed upon the face of
the dead man before him, supporting himself
upon the arm of the detective, until finally,
recovering himself, he gasped
"IT'S FATHER."

It was wrong that the family was required to buy back the elder Harrison. But that's what happened. Today the bones of John Scott Harrison, son of a president and father of another, lie in a family tomb managed by the State of Ohio.

And what of Augustus Devin? Devin's brother finally located his body far from North Bend. It took two weeks for detectives to sniff out a trail of suspicion. Thirty miles (forty-eight kilometers) due north at Miami Medical College (now Miami University in Oxford, Ohio), they found a forged signature. It hinted that Devin's body also was prepped as a cadaver. They followed up on a shipment of "pickle barrels" to the medical college at the University of Michigan in Ann Arbor and recovered him.

Today Augustus Devin's bones lie near his father's grave in the old Congress Green Cemetery.

CHAPTER SIX

HUMAN OFFERINGS HERE, THERE, AND EVERYWHERE . . .

THROUGHOUT THIS BOOK, YOU HAVE READ ABOUT examples of bony burials discovered deep beneath the feet of modern people. King Richard III was entombed under a parking lot in England. Bones have been found in the basements of medical schools.

And in Mexico City, another bony burial came to light in 2015. What archaeologists found confirmed a five-hundred-year-old rumor. A sinister story of human sacrifice that had stuck around since Spain's *conquistadores* invaded Mesoamerica.

The rumor grew from old narratives written by Spanish priests. They came with Spain's armies to force Spain's ways on a people who already ran an empire of their own. These people were the Aztecs.

Half a century after the Spanish destroyed the Aztec capital, *Tenochtitlán* (ten-oke-teet-LAHN), a Spanish priest, Father Diego Durán, wrote a history of the Aztecs. His book, now known as *The Durán Codex*, came complete with color images. One depicted a gruesome sight: *tzompantli* (tsom-PANT-lee), racks of human skulls.

Were they real? Or did the Spanish make them up in order to justify their own slaughter of others?

About 1325 CE the Aztecs established Tenochtitlán on an island in what is modern-day Mexico City. They built the grandest empire in Mesoamerica—ancient Mexico and Central America. Only the Incas in South America rivaled the Aztecs with their power and glory.

The Aztecs, who called themselves *Mexica* (MAY-hee-kah), worshipped gods and goddesses and sought their blessings. Like real people, the deities required nourishment to stay alive. It came in the form of blood, human blood. In return, the gods, among them the sun and war god, *Huitzilopochtli* (WEET-zee-lo-POKED-lee), and the rain god, *Tlaloc* (TLA-lok), shined and rained blessings on the Aztec people.

It made sense to the Aztecs to offer blood sacrifices to their gods. Prisoners of war, criminals, and ordinary women and men all qualified.

Excavation of the Templo Mayor reveals three sets of narrow steps. They are similar to the one depicted on this page (*below*) from an old manuscript about the Aztecs, attributed to the sixteenth-century Mexican Jesuit Juan de Tovar.

At Tenochtitlán's city center, there rose the *Templo Mayor* (MY-or), that mimicked a holy mountain. Its twin tops glorified Huitzilopochtli and Tlaloc. Twin sets of steep stairs ran from ground to the summit, where platforms stood for Aztec priests to slay their captives.

The priests had made ritual killing an art form. They plunged black stone knives of obsidian, edges ground sharp, into the victims' breastbones and yanked out their beating hearts. These went into special vessels, and the dead were flung down the steps. Other priests waited to decapitate them, deflesh the skulls, and drill holes in each side.

Skulls were strung like beads across wooden poles and mounted—one by one—to create *tzompantli*, those gruesome racks.

Or so the color drawings in Father Diego's book seemed to say. But did they depict the truth?

Uncovering the Templo Mayor began in 1978. An electrical worker, as he laid cable in the middle of Mexico City, made a shocking discovery. Under the ground, upon which folks had trod for centuries, lay an enormous disc of carved stone. It was the first hint of Aztec Templo Mayor, the high temple of the Aztecs. In four years archaeologists excavated

Aztec Tzompantli, a skull rack carved of stone, was unearthed at the Templo Mayor.

the magnificent shrine. The area was laid bare to twentieth-century study and preserved as a World Heritage site. But there was no sign of any skull racks.

Then in 2015 archaeologists from Mexico's National Institute of Anthropology and History (INAH) found a pile of demolished skulls in the temple complex and holes where wooden posts had once stood, suggesting a skull rack. The team deduced they had uncovered the *Huey Tzompantli* (way-yi-zoam-PANT-li), a tower of human skulls that was a monument to Huitzilopochtli. It was quite the cache.

To their surprise, experts discovered actual skulls of sacrificed people in the temple.

"A world of information," declared Raúl Barrera Rodríguez, director of INAH's Urban Archaeology Program. That world encompassed thousands of skull fragments, signs of six hundred fifty skulls, and one hundred eighty nearly complete skulls.

Back in the 1500s conquistadors had described a terrifying sight at the Templo Mayor. It was precisely the opposite for Aztecs. But why?

We don't look at human sacrifice as the Aztecs did, Dr. Rodríguez pointed out. "It is important to understand the worldview of the Aztecs. The tzompantli was about giving life."

🏠 🏠 🏠

MURDER AS A RITE

Human sacrifice. If ever two words could make you shudder, there they are.

Across history human sacrifice is on the human record. Every continent (except Antarctica, of course) has its examples of murder as ritual killing. Some anthropologists, researchers who study the development of human history, theorize that mass sacrifices took place in the most complex human societies. As cultures evolved, sacrifice expanded . . . a few here and there, then more, and thousands at once . . .

The global evidence of humans killing other humans in a ritual form begs the question "Why did people sacrifice other people?" Here's a short list of examples beyond the Aztecs:

- The Inca in South America (about 1400 CE–1532 CE)
- The Mississippians in central North America (about 700–1600 CE)
- The Vikings in northern Europe (about 800 CE–1050 CE)
- The Etruscans in Italy (about 700 BCE–50 BCE)
- The Maya in Mesoamerica (about 1500 BCE–900 CE)

- Mesopotamians in Mesopotamia (about 5000 BCE–250 BCE)
- Minoans in Crete (3000 BCE–1100 BCE)
- The Dahomey in Western Africa (about 1625 CE–1894 CE)
- Austronesians across the Pacific Ocean from Madagascar to Indonesia to Hawaii and New Zealand (about 3200 BCE–1600 CE)

By now you might have learned about the world's earliest civilizations: Egypt, the Indus Valley, China. Until the People's Republic of China was established in 1948, historians tracked its past as a series of dynasties. Among them were the Zhou, Shang, Han, and Ming, mighty families who passed their power from generation to generation.

The Shang dynasty arose about 1600 BCE and held court until 1046 BCE. Except for the work of an early Chinese scholar who wrote the first history of China about 100 BCE, we didn't know much about these early rulers until about 1930.

Animal bones pointed the way for archaeologists to find signs of the Shang people. In 1928 they began digging southwest of the modern city of Anyang in the center of Henan province. It seems they launched their venture based on an 1899 find of animal bones inscribed with some kind of

Cracks in the shoulder bone of an ox show signs of divination to predict the future.

picture writing. The project burst across an area of about three hundred fifty square miles (nine hundred square kilometers).

Today we call the area *Yinxu* (EEN-SHYOO, both in a rising tone) the "Ruins of Yin." There's evidence of eighty structures formed of earth and wooden timbers, a massive display of power and grandeur: palaces, homes, shrines, workshops. There were lovely artifacts of precious jade, bronze knives (this was the Bronze Age, don't forget), early versions of chariots, and bones. *Lots of bones of human sacrifices.*

Bones abounded in Yinxu; about thirteen thousand sacrifices have been counted. Most often these were men from age fifteen to thirty-five. When scientists did some math, they calculated that at least fifty people were killed in each sacrificial ritual. One ritual alone claimed the lives of three hundred thirty-nine victims.

In Yinxu's Royal Cemetery, a wide and sandy area, there are two kinds of burials: scores of royal ones plus more than two thousand five hundred sacrificial burial pits. Both hold the bones of sacrificed people, but they differ. In the royal graves, for instance, the victims, skeletons intact, were interred with nice stuff, and they lay among the deceased kings and others.

And why? Scientists categorized them as *rensheng* and think they were "companions in death" slaughtered to accompany a dead king or noble as a servant or relative in the next life. Their skeletons, "articulated and complete," lay on platforms as if they had had special treatment.

The bones of the *rexun* or "human offerings," those bones in the pits, showed a stark difference. They had been mutilated—"disarticulated and rarely associated with burial goods." *Disarticulated?* Pulled apart at the joints.

There are several theories about the "why" of these human sacrifices. One says that the Shang had no use for their prisoners of war, so they sacrificed them. A second suggests that the Shang went to war precisely because they needed people to sacrifice.

A third theory suggests that the Shang counted on human sacrifices to please their gods. The Shang were looking for safety and security, good weather, good health, good fortune. And so that their kings could bask in reflected glory . . . perhaps to become gods themselves.

For the record: These are theories. Some archaeologists accept one or more, but others disagree. They do laboratory research on bones and teeth to make their case, and then they share their test results in long and complicated papers.

🏠 🏠 🏠

But—and this was a big but to the Shang rulers—what exactly did their gods want from them? They turned to bones to find the answers in a process known as divination. It means to be inspired by something divine, like a god or goddess.

Shang kings did double duty as priests in order to divine the wishes of their supreme god. The process went like this:

1. Find a good-looking turtle shell or the shoulder bone of an ox.
2. Use a form of picture writing to carve wishes for military power, good harvests, and more ways to stay in charge.
3. Heat a bronze rod in a flame until it's red-hot and prod it into the turtle shell or cow shoulder until it cracks. That's a sign that the god has answers.
4. The king/priest divines, "reads," the cracks and reports the god's answers to his subjects. From what we know, only the king could do the interpreting ... how convenient.

A scholar of Chinese told me that Shang people of all classes consulted oracle bones. "Scapulomancy," he called it. A new term for me, though more people say "scapulimancy": scapula (shoulder blade) and mancy (divination).

A HIDDEN LADY

In 1976 a Chinese archaeologist, Zheng Zhenxiang, was sent to a construction site near Anyang to check it out before workers began to level the ground. These were difficult political times in China, and it was not easy for her to get permission to explore the large mound that rose from flat ground.

Zheng, who had made an educated guess about the odd sod, used a Luoyang shovel, a long open cylinder of metal, to poke holes through the soil. The tool caught soil tinged with red lacquer, a varnish-like material that dries into a shiny layer on wood or metal. It is not found naturally in the earth, so its presence pointed to something beneath the soil. The construction project stopped dead. What she found would make Zheng Zhenxiang China's "first lady of archaeology."

Zheng had tapped into the tomb of Lady Fu Hao. Long hidden, it was the only intact royal family burial from China's Shang dynasty. By Shang standards, it was only a modest burial but it was, as archaeologists say, "undisturbed." Vandals had found their way into all the rest long years ago.

We know that Lady Fu Hao was a favored wife among the many of Wu

A statue of Lady Fu Hao stands near her tomb.

Ding, a Shang king who ruled for fifty-eight years. She was said to have led armies during four wars and rounded up thirteen thousand fighters under her command. She died about 1200 BCE.

Her grave was filled with gorgeous goods of bronze—a battle ax for one—and precious jade—a jade dragon, jade parrots, and jade figures that offered clues to what Shang people looked like. There was a hairpin too. After all, this battling woman needed to keep her locks in place.

Lady Fu Hao had been encased in a wooden coffin, long rotted. But hers weren't the only bones in the burial. Zheng excavated farther, and sure enough, there were other skeletons in the pit. Sixteen human beings sacrificed to accompany the lady after death, and six dogs, too. It seems the

Shang wanted dogs with them in their graves. Puppies were especially popular.

A-VIKING FOR HUMAN SACRIFICES

Libraries are cool places. (I hope that you spend—and enjoy—time in your school or town library.) In this case, if it were not for libraries and museums that house written documents, old ones at that, we wouldn't have a clue about the Vikings and their human sacrifices.

Yes, the Vikings sacrificed other people.

This fact surprised me. I'm half Scandinavian, and I thought I knew a lot about the Vikings. At first I feared there were no bones to write about or photos to show, because Viking lore says they sent their dead leaders to sea in burning ships. But then I dug further. The Vikings did have their creepy sacrificial ways, and there are bones that prove it!

At home in Scandinavia—Denmark, Norway, and Sweden—the Vikings weren't truly "Vikings." They were farmers. But, as we learn looking up the word *víkingr* in old Germanic dictionaries, when these Nordic folk got the itch to go "a-Viking," they became pirates and other things, too. They sailed their longships from Scandinavia to wage war, settle lands, and trade goods. West to the British Isles and across the Atlantic, east to Russia and southward to the Middle East, and along the coast of western Europe, the

Vikings left their mark. As fighters and conquerors, they were a fearsome bunch.

You might have learned in school about the Vikings' belief system and how these Norse gods' names appear in modern English as "Tuesday," "Wednesday," "Thursday," and "Friday." The Vikings worshipped a panoply of gods including Thor, Woden, Odin, and Freya, and depended on them for their blessings. The lore said that when a powerful Viking warrior died, he was bestowed the high honor of having his body boarded onto a longship, set afire, and pushed out to sea. Modern blogs point out that this practice was more myth than truth.

This Viking grave—evidence of a human sacrifice—was discovered by chance before new homes were built outside Stockholm, Sweden, in the 1970s.

Still, the Vikings wrote their hopes and dreams in their sagas, *Beowulf* for one. But . . . how do we know that the Vikings sacrificed humans to their gods? That answer comes from ancient manuscripts, collections of writing before books came along that have survived for centuries.

In 1974 an archaeologist in Sweden named Ove Hemmendorf was looking into an area where new homes were to be built. First, though, there were twenty old graves to be excavated. As he told me when we met online, this was "the find of his lifetime."

> The excavation was made because the place was planned for modern house building and our task was to excavate and document and then take away all the twenty graves. Nothing indicated anything special with the place, not even the mound in which the sacrificed men were found. Just a routine excavation. When the excavation was over and done, we had not found anything special in 19 of the graves. Just ordinary things from that time. Most bodies had been cremated.
>
> But in the special one, we found these two skeletons lying in a layer of soot, charcoal, buried human and animal bones that is the common result when the dead person has been cremated in an open fire. The skeletons were very well preserved. They were lying "on their stomach" and the skulls placed anormal and turned upside down. The men seemed to have been decapitated. None of us had ever seen or heard of something like that and I called for specialists.

Soon we found that the third vertebra from the head on each of them, was cut through by a sharp tool.

Yes, the bodies had been beheaded.

After the excavation the osteologist started analyzing the skeletons, and also the burnt bones in the remains of the burying fire. The results showed that the two skeletons were from two men: one in the age of 17–22 years, the other in age 20–40. In the skull/cranium of one of them were traces of a knock [blow], which in itself could have caused his death. The other man's skull was so damaged, that such traces could not be seen.

[One] man who had been cremated had died 20–40 years old. With him in the fire had been dog, horse, and bird of some kind. Also a claw from a lynx—eventually traces of a fur/skin from a lynx. One of the skeletons has been C 14-dated and shows that he died around AD 765 /– 100. That means somewhere between 665 to 865 AD. That is early [in] the Viking age. Among the charcoal and burnt bones were also fragments of pottery and of a hair comb, some iron nails, pieces of bronze, etc. Most ordinary things we often find in cremation graves from the Viking age.

My interpretation of the find, written almost ten years after 1974 and after a lot of studies, is this:

A man 20–40 years old, living on an ordinary Viking age farm in middle Sweden, has died and his body has been placed on a cremation fire. In an ordinary way he was dressed and equipped with some things that can be useful in the time after death. No weapons such as sword or axe or the like. His horse and dog are also placed in the funeral pyre before the family puts fire to it. It burns down.

He, or his family, has decided that also two men (probably slaves/thralls in the household) shall follow the dead man to the other side. So after the fire has burnt down, the two men are being killed, decapitated with a sword. The headless bodies are laid in the burnt-down fire, close to each other but with foot and head in different directions. They are not placed on their back, as used to be the common way when burying people. Instead they are treated in a condescending way and laid on their stomach. Afterwards the heads are laid down in unnatural positions.

When this has been done, the building of the grave mound began. The two bodies are surrounded by stones that are placed in one layer upon the burnt layer of charcoal, bones, etc. Thereafter soil is thrown on the stones, until a medium high (0.75–1 m [30–39 inch]) mound is built. And that's it.

Another set of Viking sacrifices turned up in Denmark. These were of children, little kids younger than you.

Their tiny bones came to light in Trelleborg, Denmark, back in the 1930s. They were found in a group of holes that resembled sacred wells. The skeleton of one adult was there, and the bones of four children ages four to seven. At that time archaeologists did not link their deaths to any kind of Viking sacrifices.

In 1977, when a Danish farmer plowed up a heavy gold Viking neck ring beside a lake, that thinking started to change. The ring—named the "Tissø Ring" for that lake—opened the lid on a vast Viking settlement that had stood from 550 to 1050 AD.

In the early 1990s amateur archaeologists began to sweep metal detectors across the spot. They started finding jewelry and weapons, sure signs of civilization. Now the experts took notice, and every year from 1995 until 2003, archaeologists excavated the site. Among the twelve thousand objects they uncovered were bones from animal—and human—sacrifices. A large number of ritual structures and sites all were found near a chieftain's home. All these signs of rites and ceremonies began, slowly, to build up the notion of Viking sacrifice.

Those bones nudged the experts to take a new look at the Trelleborg children. And now the burial of their bodies in sacred wells started to make sense, as well. To kill a treasured child? Certainly, such a drastic step to please a Viking god would have taken place when life was very hard. Said

Lars Jørgensen, a researcher at the National Museum of Denmark:

> They [human beings] constituted the
> ultimate sacrifice, especially when children
> were involved—they only did anything
> like that if they [the Vikings] wanted to
> re-establish connections to the gods when
> things had gone seriously awry.

Awry is pronounced "aw-RYE."
Awry means amiss, off course, or just plain wrong.

CHAPTER SEVEN

BATTLES OF THE BONES AND OTHER THINGS

AMONG SCIENTISTS THERE'S A TON OF COMPETITION that demands as much energy as in sports. Take, for example, the field of anthropology, the study of human progress over the past seven million years. Anthropologists depend on physical energy to do fieldwork all over the world. And they expend mental energy in thinking about what they discover, and what their discoveries mean compared to what we already know.

Like other researchers, anthropologists put their ideas onto paper and write long, complex reports. Once all that work is finished, they send their research papers to editors at academic journals, hoping that they will be published. It's a long and tough process, rather like learning a sport and trying to make the top team at school.

Often scientists don't agree with each other. "A difference of opinion," we could say. But sometimes arguments among academics turn downright angry. Among anthropologists and paleontologists, experts who study old (very!) fossils, there have been battles of the bones . . .

HOMINID V. HOMININ

As I wrote this book, I picked up on the word *hominid* referring to our human family tree. Then I read another word, *hominin*, and I got confused. So I went to the Web, which helped clear things up. A trustworthy source, the Australian Museum, explains the difference:

This chart shows that humans (Hominini) and the great apes (Gorillini) share a common ancestor. The many skulls at top denote what is known about the evolution of humans.

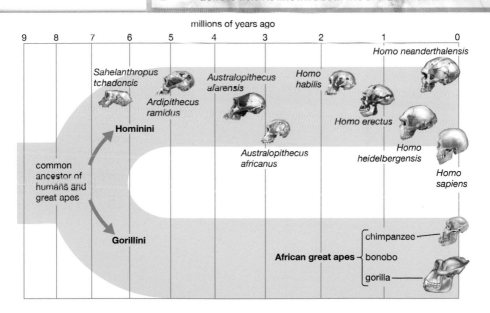

Hominid—the group consisting of all modern and extinct Great Apes (that is, modern humans, chimpanzees, gorillas and orangutans plus all their immediate ancestors).

Hominin—the group consisting of modern humans, extinct human species and all our immediate ancestors (including members of the genera *Homo, Australopithecus, Paranthropus* and *Ardipithecus*).

The museum tells readers that *hominid* used to mean the human line *only*, but that has changed. When you read more about the human line, check the date of your source.

You probably know that you, your family, and every person on earth are members of *homo sapiens*, or human beings. *Homo sapiens*, our species, means "wise man."

In short:

The hominids are all of the great ape family, humans included.

The hominid line splits into two branches: Group 1 contains orangutans, and Group 2 includes everybody else, which is gorillas, chimps, and humans.

Group 2 then splits into three new branches: one for gorillas, one for chimps, and one for us. We humans have our own branch, the hominins.

🏛 🏛 🏛

When you compare humans with the rest of the great apes, you can understand why we are different. We are not covered

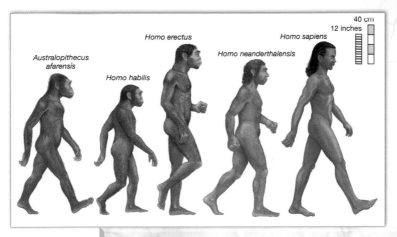

Australopithecus
afarensis

Homo habilis

Homo erectus

Homo neanderthalensis

Homo sapiens

40 cm
12 inches

An artist's depiction of five species, part of the human lineage

in fur. Unlike apes we cannot climb trees very easily because our feet have evolved in a different way. We are *bipedal*; we walk on two feet. Most of the time, apes walk on four feet using their back legs and their hands in a scrambling gait.

Our brains are nearly three times larger than the brains of great apes. Another human quality: Our brains are organized to help us use tools. Yes, you might say, but chimps use tools, too. But that's only in a limited way. Humans have evolved to use and create tools from sharp rocks, the hand ax, and pottery bowls all the way to the minicomputer in your hand that you call a "cell phone."

Finally, we can talk. Besides body language, we humans use spoken language and written language. Think about that! What have we as human beings been able to accomplish because we have the skills with language?

How do we understand all this human development? By bones in the fossil record.

🏛 🏛 🏛

Imagine the excitement when news filtered out from Africa in 1974, where a unique set of fossils came to light in Ethiopia. A young paleontologist named Donald Johanson, fresh out of graduate school, had made his first trip to Hadar in Ethiopia. Quite without warning, he came across a shoulder bone that looked humanlike. Yet he thought it was not part of the evolutionary line that led to *homo sapiens*, a modern human.

Johanson and another researcher, Tom Gray, unearthed about forty percent of the skeletal remains of this small creature. Its pelvic bones, shaped for pregnancy, hinted that it was female. He carefully considered the little hominin that lay before him and decided rather quickly to name it *Australopithecus afarensis*. That's Latin for "southern ape from afar." Afar is indeed a place, but it's also very far from most of us.

As Johanson's group gathered around an evening campfire, someone played a cassette tape of the Beatles hit album *Sgt. Pepper's Lonely Hearts Club Band*. Along came the track "Lucy in the Sky with Diamonds." That very night, the tiny primate had her name.

Lucy became a rock star. Word of Johanson's discovery made the papers and nightly news programs.

But the academic world of anthropology and paleontology was set, as they say, on its ear. Johanson's theory outright contradicted the work of a respected family, the Leakeys. Louis and Mary Leakey had pioneered paleontology in Africa, looking for and studying fossilized human skeletons. Now their son Richard, who followed in his parents' bipedal footsteps, said that Johanson was wrong.

A copy of Lucy is on display in the National Museum of Ethiopia.

The Leakey family was practically royalty among anthropologists. Louis Leaky had been a flashy outlier, and other anthropologists thought he wasn't a careful scientist. Leakey had worked in the Olduvai Gorge, now in the country of Tanzania.

Leakey and his team had found a different fossil group. Starting only with the hand and foot bones of a twelve-year-old specimen, he had worked tirelessly to find and categorize more fossil evidence of this new species.

As researchers do, Leakey and others had published a paper in 1964 in the science journal *Nature*. He boldly announced the little creature's scientific name, *Homo habilis,* or "handy man." Leakey stated that *his* fossil bones were members of the human family: "*homo*-this or *homo*-that."

Leakey's thinking had stretched the human family line much farther back in history. He stated his reasons. These small prehumans had:

- bigger skulls to protect bigger brains
- smaller teeth in the back of their jaws
- feet that looked more like our human feet than ape feet, AND
- hands that could use tools*

Like father, like son. Richard Leakey, miles from where his father had worked, made his own discovery in 1972. Fragments had been pieced into a skull that had enclosed a brain of forty-six cubic inches (nine hundred fifty cubic centimeters). Richard Leakey described the owner of this skull as a member of *Homo habilis*. Then in 1975, his mother, Mary Leakey, found fossils in Laetoli, Tanzania, that she labeled *Homo habilis*, too.

All their discoveries of *Homo habilis* set the Leakeys on one side of the academic argument.

All over Africa, there was plenty of fossil evidence of *Australopithecus*, too. And that begged the question "Had Donald Johanson been too quick to label Lucy as a brand-new species?"

*Stone tools were scattered among the fossil bones.

Johanson and his colleague paleoanthropologist Tim White didn't think so.

Without question, Johanson said, Lucy was a common ancestor who walked the earth before two other groups: *Australopithecus*,

In 1977, Richard Leakey posed with skulls from two species: Australopithecus was in his right hand, and Homo habilis in his left hand.

whose line died out, and *Homo-*, the line that led to us. He placed Lucy and her kin among the "*australopithecines.*"

In 1981 the feuding fossil finders taped a television program hosted by Walter Cronkite on CBS. Richard Leakey and Johanson arrived at the studio, clearly postured for a disagreement. Cronkite, famously respected for his interview skills, expected to ask Johanson and Leakey general questions. But the meeting sped downhill as their egos surged. Johanson produced a chart showing his version of where Lucy stood. He handed Leakey a marker and invited him to draw *his* version.

Meanwhile, Johanson turns to the camera to begin an explanation, . . . of what in fact the differences of opinion are. Leakey interrupts, asks Johanson to hold one edge of

the chart, and says, "I think I would probably
do that," and he places a large X through
Johanson's carefully drawn tree. "Well, what
would you draw in its place?" challenges
Johanson, who is visibly taken aback by
Leakey's action. Regaining his composure
somewhat, Leakey says, "A question mark,"
and does so boldly, filling his
allotted space . . .

Meanwhile, a new technique for studying fossil bones was
evolving as well. Scientists had made big strides in genetics,
learning how DNA works in our cells and how parents pass
on their traits to their offspring. Thanks to genetic studies on fossils, scientists mostly agree that apes and humans
diverged and went their separate ways from six to eight million years ago.

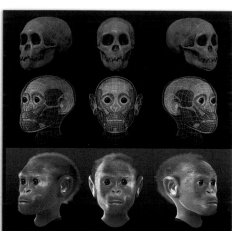

A facial reconstruction of Taung Child, a young member of Lucy's species

Experts now say that the *Homo-* line evolved until modern humans, *Homo sapiens*, appeared. We emerged in Africa about three hundred thousand years ago. The Leakeys had been correct about Africa as our ancestral home. And Donald Johanson had placed Lucy correctly on our ancestry chart.

Think! Eight million years ago. Three hundred thousand years ago.

Homo sapiens is the new kid on the block.

This story about Donald Johanson and Richard Leakey has a happy ending. The two met again in front of an audience in

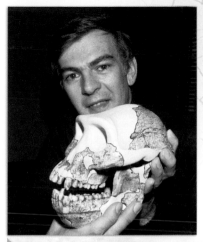

Donald Johanson holds a model of Lucy's skull in 1981. Lucy's brain was about one-fifth larger than that of a chimp.

2011. This time the mood was chill, as if two mighty lions had made peace and agreed to disagree about the details. Johanson and Leakey shared the message that studying the human past is incredibly and indelibly important.

Kids look at a model of Lucy in the National Museum of Anthropology and History in Mexico City.

As Richard Leakey affirmed. "I think if we can make it understood and clear that, irrespective of superficial features, we all are one people and we owe it to each other to respect each as one species, one people with one origin."

And catch this: In 2008 this piece of news had appeared in the *New York Times*:

CRADLE OF HUMANKIND, South Africa— Nine-year-old Matthew Berger dashed after his dog, Tau, into the high grass here one sunny morning, tripped over a log and stumbled onto a major archaeological discovery. Scientists announced Thursday that he had found the bones of a new hominid species that lived almost two million years ago during the fateful, still mysterious period spanning the emergence of the human family.

"Dad, I found a fossil!" Matthew said he cried out to his father, Lee R. Berger, an American paleoanthropologist, who had been searching for hominid bones just a hill and a half away for almost two decades . . .

NEANDERTHALS GROW FLOWER POWER

After working for nearly five years in the Kurdish part of Iraq, a team of archaeologists in 2020 heralded a new find. "The first articulated Neanderthal skeleton to come out of the ground in southwest Asia for over twenty years" was discovered in Shanidar Cave. Dr. Emma Pomeroy, an

To this day, plant life abounds outside the entrance to Shanidar Cave.

archaeologist from the University of Cambridge in England, worked with the team.

"It's almost the entire top half of a body from the waist upwards," she said.

"We've got the skull, we've got the left arm and hand fairly complete, the right shoulder and the right hand, then the spinal column down to about the waist level and all of the ribs as well."

Just as cool was where the bones were buried—right beyond the stopping point of an earlier excavation that took place in that same wide-mouthed cave in 1960. Back then, an archaeologist named Ralph Solecki excavated a chunk of sediment one meter square (thirty-nine by thirty-nine inches) that was transferred on top of a taxi to a museum in Baghdad. The sediment held the remains of a male and fragments from three other skeletons.

Inside, Shanidar Cave is a busy spot for archaeologists.

This time battles about the bones blossomed into something different. The controversy was about . . . flowers! Dr. Solecki and pollen expert Arlette Leroi-Gourhan noted that flower pollen (the stuff that makes you sneeze) ringed the bony remains. Where there was pollen there had been flowers, all around the body of the dead male. Solecki theorized that this particular Neanderthal had been buried with emotion and ritual, just as people honor their dead today.

Since the first Neanderthal fossils were discovered in 1829, for many years, science had viewed Neanderthals as sluggish, stupid creatures. Their skeletons seemed to say that they had stooped posture, heavy bones, and apelike faces. Some doubted that Neanderthals, whose bones had been discovered both in the cold parts of Europe and in Southwest Asia, belonged in the *Homo* family at all. Therefore, any hints that a Neanderthal was buried with flowers—or even formally buried at all—meant that they were far more humanlike than anyone had thought. FYI ... it's "nee-AN-der-TAL."

The Old Man of La Chappelle

In 1908 the first full skeleton of a Neanderthal had been discovered in a La Chapelle-aux-Saints cave in France. "The Old Man of La Chapelle" sported a classic Neanderthal face with its pushed-back forehead, a pair of heavy brow ridges, and a midface that jutted out. The French expert who first reconstructed the skeleton imagined him as a bent-over, stumbling creature that had little in common with *Homo sapiens*.

But the Old Man was re-examined several times over the next one hundred years, and new views of him took hold. For one a 1950s study concluded that the poor fellow was truly old among his kind, at the age of forty no less. He had suffered—greatly—from "gross deforming osteoarthritis." In other words he was bent over and hurting exactly as many older people are today!

More recently another scholar decided that the original researcher had made a big mistake based on his biases, ideas that he held beforehand. As already mentioned, those

A facial model of a Neanderthal

1900s viewpoints said that Neanderthals had no place near us in the human family tree.

We now know that he was wrong.

🏠 🏠 🏠

But back to those flowers. Other experts did their own studies of plant pollen in Shanidar Cave and concluded that today, pollen is pretty much everywhere. Animals could have brought pollen into their burrows in the cave, or Neanderthals could have tracked pollen in on their feet. Heck, even the wind could blow pollen into a cave! But Dr. Leroi-Gourhan was convinced the only explanation for the pattern of pollen around the body was the deliberate placement of flowers, and scientists still debate this today.

In 2015 when the Cambridge researchers were first granted permission to excavate the cave, could anyone envision that they would find more bones? "In fact, the project never set out to find more bones and didn't expect to!" Dr. Pomeroy remarked. There were big areas of sediment (think sand, silt, and small rocks) for the team to remove as it worked through a trench in the cave.

The next year they found a rib, the bones of a clenched right hand, and then a lumbar vertebra, a backbone. In 2018 and 2019 they found a skull "flattened by thousands of years

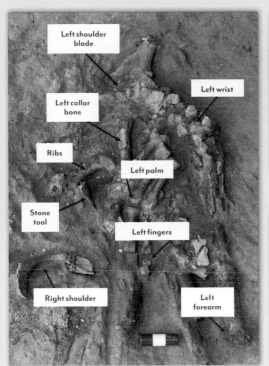

Left shoulder blade

Left wrist

Left collar bone

Ribs

Left palm

Stone tool

Left fingers

Right shoulder

Left forearm

Multiple bones of Shanidar Z

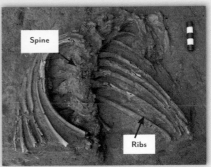

Spine

Ribs

Shanidar Z's torso, showing part of the spine and ribs

Eye

Mouth

Shanidar Z's crushed skull

Shanidar Z was unearthed over several seasons of excavation.

of sediment." More bones from the upper body appeared, as well as a left hand that seemed to cradle the skull from underneath.

The team has dated the skeleton, officially named Shanidar Z, to about seventy thousand years old. Today they are still looking for evidence of flower pollen at the same burial site. That said, it's a burial for sure. Professor Graeme Barker from Cambridge's McDonald Institute for Archaeological Research made that clear. "The new excavation suggests that some of these bodies were laid in a channel in the cave floor created by water, which had then been intentionally dug to make it deeper ... There is strong early evidence that Shanidar Z was deliberately buried."

🏛 🏛 🏛

THE BATTLE FOR KENNEWICK MAN

Two teens had a big surprise in southeastern Washington when they stumbled upon a human skull in a shallow part of the Columbia River near the Oregon border. Their discovery in 1996 thrilled archaeologists and anthropologists across the United States and more.

Dr. Doug Owsley led the research, as he had with "Jane," the young woman whose skull was found at Jamestown.

This set of bones was one of the very few skeletons of an ancient person to appear in the Western Hemisphere.

A copy of Kennewick Man's skull

The team used osteobiology, a "biography of the bones," to help them tell the dead man's tale. From the looks of things, he had walked the earth about nine thousand years ago. He stood five feet seven inches (one and seven-tenths meters) tall and weighed about one hundred sixty pounds (seventy-three kilos).

Marks on the shoulder bones (where tendons attached them to muscles) showed he'd been a right-hander. He'd lived to about age forty, and sometime during his life he'd been hit in the chest, as his five still-broken ribs proved. Not only that . . . he had two small fractures in his cranium—and a stone arrowhead in his hip. "One tough dude," wrote Douglas Preston for *Smithsonian* magazine.

The tough dude was dubbed "Kennewick Man" for where he'd been discovered.

The researchers wanted to investigate the stone arrowhead; its chemical composition could offer clues where Kennewick Man had spent his days. But the U.S. Army Corps of Engineers, who managed the river where the skeleton was found, said no. The bones went into storage.

🏛 🏛 🏛

After all of this amazing information-gathering, shouldn't Kennewick Man go on display in a museum of natural history? That had been the practice for many years. But not everyone approved. Indigenous Americans, people whom you might know as "Native Americans" or "American Indians," saw this practice as dead wrong.

It was no secret that for years, their burial grounds had been robbed of bodies and goods known as "funerary objects." Sometimes the graves were new, but others were much older—what we think of as prehistoric. Often the bones of the dead were tossed aside. Some ended up labeled and cataloged in jumbled drawers or boxes in universities and museums.

Later in the 1900s voices of America's indigenous people rang out in anger: The bodies of their dead had been abused and disrespected. No matter that a dead person was laid to rest on a platform in a tree, left exposed to the wind and weather on an icefield, or buried in a mound of earth—*the dead were to be left alone.*

The U.S. Congress passed a bill that was signed into law in 1990. The Native American Graves Protection and Repatriation Act made it clear that "human remains and other cultural items removed from federal or tribal lands belong, in the first instance, to lineal descendants, Indian tribes, and Native Hawaiian organizations." In other words, bodies of their dead ancestors were the property of indigenous Americans.

Kennewick Man served as but one example of the long-standing problem. In Bloomington, Illinois, in 2006, a woman went into the attic of the old home she'd bought and was horrified to find a cabinet of thirty skulls of indigenous people. Some were inked with "Lake Anderson Mounds 1933." Apparently, a town dentist had removed them from an ancient burial site that was at least one thousand years old. The police took charge of the skulls and, out of respect for the beliefs of their Native American descendants, refused permission for them to be photographed.

The skull and bones of Kennewick Man became the focus of an ugly public debate that unfolded over twenty years. Researchers sued the U.S. government in order to make a brief study of the bones. Meanwhile, members of five Native American tribes demanded that "the Ancient One," their name for him, be returned to them and buried. In time DNA tests showed that Kennewick Man did have a genetic link to the Colville tribe in the Pacific Northwest.

The Ancient One was repatriated to those who wanted to bury him, and bury him they did in a secret spot.

The whole episode was long and painful for everyone— indigenous Americans, and scientists, museums, and others who were deeply curious about Kennewick Man and what stories his bones could tell.

But one truth did arise from this battle for his bones. It was time for archaeologists and other researchers to consult with indigenous groups when they hoped to investigate a Native burial site. That did happen in

Paleontologists Tim Heaton (*right*) and Dave Love in 1994 investigating Bumper Cave, located on northern Prince of Wales, Alaska, near Shuká Káa Cave. Bumper Cave contained ten brown bear skeletons dating between approximately 6,800 and 11,500 years old.

Jonathan Rowan Jr., the Master Carver for the City of Klawock on Prince of Wales Island, holds the bone box he created to entomb the remains of Shuká Káa.

Alaska—and at the same time when the battle over Kennewick Man took place.

On Prince of Wales Island, Dr. Tim Heaton, a paleontologist, was excavating a cave in a remote area of the Tongass National Forest in 1996. He found the cave rich in the remains of Ice Age mammals. Unexpectedly, a scattering of ancient bones of a young man's jaw, vertebrae, hip, and a few ribs appeared as Heaton was working on July 4.

The rescarchers stopped digging immediately and reported the discovery of the human bones to the Forest Service. The agency reached out to the indigenous people who lived in the area, and they began to talk and share ideas. The island tribes, representatives from the U.S. Forest Service, and the researchers came to an agreement that the remains should be studied first and then buried. Only one man's remains were found in the cave. Eventually (twelve years later) they named him Shuká Káa, which translates as "The Man Ahead of Us" or "The Man Before Us," and the place where he was found came to be called Shuká Káa Cave.

Shuká Káa was thought to have lived about ten thousand eight hundred years ago. The experts who examined him speculated that he had died while hunting, and that scavenger animals had disturbed his bones.

After a joyful celebration shared by the island tribes, the Forest Service, and the scientists who had learned from him, Shuká Káa was reburied on Prince of Wales Island in September 2008.

Terry Fifield, an archaeologist for the U.S. Forest Service, was part of the group that worked together to honor Shuká Káa. Many years on, he thought back about the experience:

> It was inspiring to see so many different people, from different walks of life come to appreciate the knowledge gained through the study of Shuká Káa. The idea, expressed by several Alaska Native participants, that an ancestor had given himself to teach us all about the past, felt right. With reburial I had a sense of calm and felt we had all acted with respect.

FACTLET

WHAT TO DO IF YOU FIND HUMAN BONES

MR. TERRY FIFIELD, who helped me find information about Shuká Káa, worked and lived with his family on Prince of Wales Island in Alaska for twenty years. When I spoke with him, he asked if I'd written anything about what to do if you randomly discover bones. I had not, and he generously offered to provide this information.

FINDING BONES in the wilds is a real possibility in many parts of the world. It can be exciting to make such a discovery. But that excitement comes with a responsibility not to damage the value associated with the remains. We have to recognize that the presence of the bones in the woods may hold information about events that occurred in the recent or ancient past. The bones may be related to a missing person case. Their presence may result from looting or disturbance of a grave site or cemetery. They may be part of a prehistoric archaeological site and have the potential to provide valuable information about ancient people's lives. Our ability to learn about the past, recent or ancient, depends on how the remains are handled beginning with when they are discovered.

If you think you have stumbled on human bones your first responsibility is to treat them as if they are part of a crime scene, a recent death or even murder. You should not touch anything or move anything. If you have a digital camera or cell phone with you, taking a few photos of the bones and of the area where you found them will likely be useful. Taking notes in a scientific manner is always a good idea. As quickly as possible you should report your discovery to the appropriate law enforcement agency. That might be the park ranger if you're in a national or state park, a district ranger if you're in a national forest, the state troopers, or the local police.

It is law enforcement's responsibility to determine if the remains represent a crime scene (are forensic) or fall in the historic or archaeological realm. Forensic anthropologists working at the direction of local, state, or federal government will determine if the remains are Native American or not. If they are Native American, the government agency has the responsibility of notifying and consulting with potentially affiliated tribes.

In many cases chance discoveries of human remains by hikers and campers can lead to important research and new understandings of events that happened in the past. Remember the hikers in the Tyrolean Alps who reported Ötzi? (Ötzi is the frozen mummy spotted by a husband and wife during a hike high on a mountain.) Those studies are most productive when new discoveries are reported quickly, and archaeologists are presented with an undisturbed puzzle with as many intact pieces as possible.

FACTLET

HOW TO BECOME A FOSSIL

FOSSILIZED BONES. I HOPE you have seen some. At my Greater Cincinnati Airport, we have fossilized skeletons of a giant sloth and a dire wolf that greet passengers.

When do bones become fossils? It takes a while. A long while, at least ten thousand years. How likely is it for any living thing to end up fossilized? An animal or human bone has *a one-tenth chance in one million* of becoming a fossil.

Paleontologists explain why. First, boney remains need protection. When a polar bear dies in the frozen north, or a camel passes on in the desert, likely their carcasses decompose in those harsh conditions. Flesh decays or is eaten by scavengers. Bones are exposed to cold, wind, salt water, and ice or to heat, wind, sand, and sun, and they wear away. In more moderate climates, buried bones disintegrate over time, as well.

The best examples of fossils are bones that Mother Nature covered up in a hurry after an animal or human died. It could be sediment dumped by flood waters, or mud and ash from volcanic explosions, and so on. Then Mother Nature works her magic. The American Museum of Natural History in New York tells us:

> Over millions of years, water in the nearby rocks surrounds these hard parts, and minerals in the water replace them, bit by bit. When the minerals have completely replaced the organic tissue, what's left is a solid rock copy of the original specimen.

CHAPTER EIGHT

SHAFTED

OLD MINES AND WELLS HAVE PROVED TO BE CONVENIENT grave sites. Prehumans, murderous politicians, and city fathers all have relied on underground shafts to stash the bodies of the dead.

HOMICIDE BY HOMININ

The following breaking news hit the inboxes of scientists everywhere in late May 2015.

> Here we report the earliest evidence of lethal interpersonal violence in the hominin fossil record. Cranium 17 recovered from the *Sima de los Huesos* Middle Pleistocene site shows two clear perimortem depression fractures on the

frontal bone, interpreted as being produced by two episodes of localized blunt force trauma.

That's quite a mouthful! Scholars and researchers write in precise language in order to make very clear what they want to say. That said, there's a less formal, but perfectly acceptable way to say the same thing to a general audience like you and me:

> We are here to tell you that we have discovered the first evidence ever of murder in the ancestral line of human beings. Skull Number 17, located in the *Sima de los Huesos* (Pit of Bones), an archaeological site in Spain, dates back to the Middle Pleistocene Era, about four hundred thirty thousand years. Skull Number 17 shows two holes in the forehead above the left eye socket. We believe that this individual died from blunt force trauma.

Perhaps you have read or heard of "blunt force trauma." Coroners' reports to police and courts use the term, which often involves head injuries from accidents, falls, explosions, or being hit by blunt objects. A bat, wrench, hammer, golf club, even a rock.

The Gran Dolina site at Atapuerca in the mountains of northern Spain is rich with remains of early hominids, caves discovered in 1976. To paleontologists and archaeologists,

The site of Gran Dolina in Atapuerca, Spain, in 2008. Beneath the platform at bottom of photo, a woman in a red shirt is excavating human bones.

Atapuerca is a wonderland. Its earliest fossil record (bits of jawbone and teeth) of the human line reaches back between one million one hundred thousand to one million two hundred thousand years.

In one cave a deep pit held a clay-covered pile of bones. These remains predate Neanderthals with their prominent midfaces and thick fingers, but not quite what you'd picture as a fully formed Neanderthal. In all, the pit held at least twenty-eight corpses. As sediment piled up on top of them, their skulls had shattered.

The skull of the possible murder victim had broken into fifty-two pieces. A team of experts in fossils, biology, and human history put them together. Reassembled, the skull itself became a puzzle that blew their minds.

Just above the left eye were two holes that didn't look like damage from the fall down the pit. A computed tomography (CT) scanner offered up more than one thousand x-ray images, rather like slices in a loaf of bread. From these the researchers created a three-dimensional model of the skull, ready for study. They decided that this skull had belonged to a young individual but didn't know its gender.

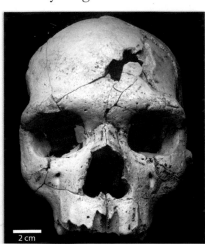

2 cm

Cranium 17, with holes in the forehead, hints that this person was murdered, because there was no sign of healing.

To their expert eyes, the twin fractures looked suspicious. The archaeologists and paleontologists already knew what happens to dead bodies dropped into pits and left there for months—or centuries. They ruled out these "taphonomic" processes—how the bones became fossilized.

The researchers used the same forensic techniques

that police detectives use to study the bodies of the dead. Forensic experts sort cranial trauma, head injuries, into different categories. "Accidental or unintentional trauma typically affects the sides of the cranial vault [the chamber that holds the brain], while intentional injuries are more commonly found in the facial region."

- Falls are usually associated with generalized cranial trauma, which tends to produce large linear fractures, especially at the level of the "hat brim line."
- Although cranial depression fractures can be a consequence of accidents, they are more likely to be the result of interpersonal violence.
- In the case of Cr-17 (Cranium 17) it is also possible to rule out the injuries as either self-inflicted or resulting from an unintentional hunting accident, mainly because the lesions (injuries) involve multiple blows.

Finally, the team said this:

> Based on the absence of cut marks, other potential postmortem manipulations (e.g., cannibalism, ritual manipulations, etc.) seem even less likely and more speculative.

In other words, the team rejected any thoughts that this individual had been sacrificed or eaten in some kind of ceremony.

Given the age of the fossilized remains, this human ancestor represents the earliest clear case of "deliberate, lethal interpersonal aggression in the hominin fossil record."

Plainly, he or she was murdered.

The researchers had more to say about the other hominins who dropped this one down the shaft. It was clear that s/he was dead before the inelegant burial. This got the investigators thinking. S/he shared the grave with many more who were dumped there, as well. Was this typical behavior for the group? Is this how prehumans dealt with their dead? What did it all mean?

Perhaps time will tell.

THE ROMANOVS—RE-MEMBERING THE RUSSIAN ROYALS

So that you are clear on what you read next, here's a brief rundown of events in Russia about one hundred years ago:

Like all major world powers, Russia has a troubled and bloody history. In 1914 it joined France and Great Britain to fight Germany and Austria-Hungary. Now we know this fearsome conflict as "World War I."

But back home in Russia, life for ordinary people was very tough. Peasants in the countryside and factory workers in cities were hungry, poor, and disrespected. With the chaos of war playing in the background, their leaders demanded an end to the monarchy. The Russian army turned against the emperor, Tsar Nicholas II, and refused to back him. Nicholas had no choice but to abdicate—step down from—his throne.

Who would lead Russia, the largest country in the world? No one could agree. A struggle for power followed, but in November 1917, a political group named the Bolsheviks seized control of the government.

The Bolsheviks claimed to represent peasants, workers, and foot soldiers. Vladimir Lenin led their Communist Party, nicknamed the "Reds." For Russia, World War I ended when Lenin signed a treaty with Germany in March 1918. But the treaty set Lenin's opponents, the "Whites," against Lenin and the Bolsheviks. Instead of a war against Germany, the Red Army and the White Army battled each other in a civil war. They fought all across Russia from the Barents Sea to the Pacific Ocean. In 1920 Lenin's Communist Party won. They renamed Russia the Union of Soviet Socialist Republics (USSR). The Soviets ruled until 1989.

🏠 🏠 🏠

And when the tsar abdicated, every member of the royal family was put to death by its own government. There was the father, Tsar Nicholas II; his wife, Tsarina Alexandra; their son and heir, Tsarevich Alexei; and four daughters: Grand Duchess Maria, Grand Duchess Olga, Grand

Duchess Tatiana, and Grand Duchess Anastasia. All grand names and titles for a royal family, but a family, nonetheless.

The family's last name was "Romanov." The Romanovs had ruled Russia for three hundred years. The sordid story of their murders shocked the world.

Lenin's Communist Party—the Reds—forced the ex-tsar and his family to live in disgrace. The Russian royals were denied safe passage to their royal relatives in western Europe. Instead, the government put them on a train to Siberia, the same cold and bleak region where the Romanovs had sent their political prisoners—about as far from civilization as possible.

Nicholas II of Russia with the family (*left to right*): Olga, Maria, Nicholas II, Alexandra, Anastasia, Alexei, and Tatiana.

At first the family lived in relative comfort in an estate home. They kept their servants and were allowed to go to church. Their family physician, Dr. Eugene Botkin, was on hand. He was essential, because young Alexei was very sick with hemophilia, a bleeding disorder. Often his father had to carry the young, weak teen in his arms.

But as the Bolsheviks overpowered their enemies, life got far rougher for the Romanovs. The family was forced to move to Ekaterinburg, another Siberian city, into a house much less grand. Outside the town the White Army was preparing to stage an invasion. The Russian royal family was sure to be freed if the White Army got a hold on them.

The Bolsheviks hated any notions of monarchy, and they took out their hate on the Romanovs. Windows were painted over, and meals were served as their Bolshevik guards sat beside the family and grubbed food from the table. The guards drew caricatures of the parents and dirty poems on the walls and taunted the girls in a vulgar way.

In the early hours of July 18, 1918, the tsar was

Grand Duchess Tatiana at work in the garden where the family was imprisoned awakened by his Bolshevik guards and told he was being removed with his family to a new location. Every member woke up and dressed for the journey in their traveling out-fits. Three maids and Dr. Botkin readied themselves, too. They were herded into the cellar to wait for their carriages. As their guard explained, the family would out be out of harm's way in case the White Army should come near.

Twelve armed Bolsheviks entered that cellar room. Their leader, a member of Lenin's secret police named Jankel Jurovsky, confronted the tsar and read a political proclamation from the paper he held. Jurovsky pulled out a pistol and shot Nicholas through the chest.

Bursts of gunfire echoed across the tight room. Bullets found their mark and killed Tsarina Alexandra outright. The guards' bullets literally bounced off jewels secretly sewn in the girls' clothing and did not kill them. Young Alexei lay wounded on top of his parents' bodies, and Jurovsky shot him dead. The guards bayoneted anyone who was still alive. The terror lasted for twenty minutes.

The cellar in that Ekaterinburg house was a mess of screams, blood, and death.

The murderers threw the dead family on a truck and transported them twelve kilometers to a forest near a small village. Jurovsky was fierce in his plan that there should be no trace of the dead royals, not ever. Their traveling clothes were pulled from their corpses. Layers of precious jewels appeared in the daughters' underclothing. Jurovsky's men poured acid over their faces to obliterate them all, dismembered them, dumped gasoline over everything, and set it afire.

The villagers knew that something very suspicious had taken place. They later testified that they had seen the light from the forest shine bright at night and all through the next day. The villagers hid until Jurovsky and his men left the area and then headed into the woods. The killers had dumped the burned bodies down an old mine shaft. They had tried to leave the area looking like picnickers had built a fire there.

This had been no picnic. In the cinders and soil ,the villagers found belt buckles of father and son, six sets of corset steels the women had worn, buckles from their shoes, and hooks and eyes from their underclothing. They also found

... the broken lenses of the Empress's eyeglasses; a set of artificial teeth identified as those of Dr. Botkin; fragments of chopped and sawed human bones; and one human finger, long, slender, well-shaped, probably cut from the Empress's hand to get at a ring.

Eggshells, of all things, left a trace, too. The killers had needed something to eat, and Jurovsky had placed an order of hard-boiled eggs to feed them.

It didn't take long for word of the family's slaughter to seep out of Siberia. As the White Army closed in on Ekaterinburg, the Bolsheviks fled. But in the end the White Army lost to the "Reds," and Vladimir Lenin ruled the USSR.

We now know that the Bolsheviks retrieved the burned remains of the Romanovs and reburied them in a spot called Pig's Meadow. They lay there until 1979.

The government tried to rub the royal family out of the national memory. In time every Russian who had lived under Nicholas II died. The Romanovs were gone but not totally forgotten.

🏠 🏠 🏠

Then, as always, times changed. As with so many crimes, the Romanovs' bones told the truth.

In 1979 Geli Ryabov, a filmmaker with the Soviet Ministry of Internal Affairs, with the help of a local geologist, Aleksandr Avdonin, went looking for signs of the family's long-abandoned graves. Clues led them to Pig's Meadow, and there they found evidence of nine human beings, including three skulls and fragments of bone. But the political atmosphere was still cold and closed. The discovery stayed quiet until 1989, when a new Russian leader named Mikhail Gorbachev turned the USSR toward openness and change.

In a complex series of tests and more tests using DNA from the bones and genetic tests of living family members,

scientists confirmed that
the nine sets of remains
were those of Nicholas,
Alexandra, Tatiana, Olga,
and Anastasia, as well as of
Dr. Botkin and three house
servants. The government,
now renamed Russia,
accepted the research
reports as truth. With
great ceremony, the five
royals were entombed in
a family crypt in their old
palace in St. Petersburg.

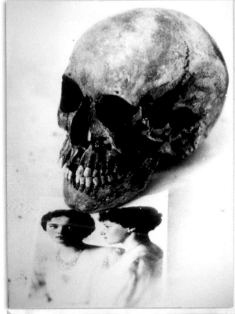

The skull of one of the daughters of the
Romanov family

And yet there were two
children missing. The bones of Alexei and Maria were not
among the jumble of ashes and bones at Pig's Meadow. In
2007 an American search group returned to Pig's Meadow
and found another bone pit with two more sets of remains.
Again the forensic specialists went to work on the fragments and verified that these were, in fact, the bones of the
missing youngsters.

🏛 🏛 🏛

This long and aching story is still political and dragging on.
In mid-2020 when this chapter was written, the bones of
Alexei and Maria had not yet been laid to rest with the rest
of the Romanovs.

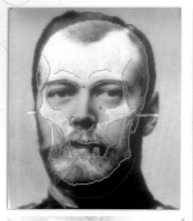

Forensic researchers used photographic superimposition to examine Tsar Nicholas II's skull.

The skull and upper skeleton of Tsar Nicholas II

SKULLDUGGERY IN PARIS

It is axiomatic that cities outgrow their cemeteries. It has happened in the United States in spots like Boston and Philadelphia, which were founded in 1630 and 1682, respectively. Can you imagine what happens to the bodies of the dead in much older cities?

Take Paris, France, for one. Paris has been around since 250 to 200 BCE, and by the Middle Ages was a model for medieval capitals in the 1200s. Roman Catholic churches had served the faithful since 500 AD, and the faithful dead were buried nearby in sacred ground.

As the years piled on, so did the numbers of graves therein, and there lay the problem. By the 1100s Paris's main cemetery, Holy Innocents' Cemetery, was in need of a new tall wall to encircle not only its original burial chambers, but also mass graves of fifteen hundred people. Did these unfortunates die of famine or pestilence?

More people were born and died in the next four hundred years. To make room for these dead, the former residents of Holy Innocents' Cemetery were disinterred—dug up. Their bones were dumped into so-called charnel houses, arched chambers newly added along those old walls.

Another three hundred years passed, and by the 1700s, the Holy Innocents' Cemetery was filthy and disgusting. A charnel house wall collapsed during heavy rains and spilled bones everywhere.

In 1780 King Louis XIV decreed that the cemetery was forever closed, as were all graveyards within the city limits. The plotting went even further, as plans were made to move all of the cemetery's residents to a string of old limestone quarries in the burbs of Paris. Under cover of night, wagonloads of bones were hauled to the old mine, where they were sent belowground down a pair of old wells.

Workers in the old mines shifted the shafted bones to a few select spots and piled them up for maximum use of space. The site became Paris's official ossuary, a giant container of bones. Not to mention a kind of exhibit, because many of the skulls and bones were laid to rest with an artful touch. To Parisian sensibilities, it made sense for the ossuary to open to tourists beginning in 1809. With a nod to ancient Rome, those in charge called them the "Catacombs of Paris."

You can visit today, provided that you follow the rules on the site's website:

PROHIBITIONS

A bit of discipline never hurt anyone!

To ensure preservation of the site, you must not eat or

drink on the site circuit, and animals are not allowed.

And, of course, you must not touch the bones, which

are the fragile remains of millions of Parisians.

Paris's city center changed even more in the 1800s. Architects drew plans with nineteenth-century trends. The old cemetery and its ancient church vanished beneath them.

Mon Dieu! (My goodness!)

Skulls line a pathway through the Catacombs of Paris. The sign says "Bones from the Cemetery of the Innocents deposited in October 1787."

CHAPTER NINE

BONES AND BENEVOLENCE

BURIALS OF THE DEAD STRETCH BACK TO EARLY HUMANS and Neanderthals, too. A burial or cremation is a sign that we care about others and honor their lives. When we uncover archaeological evidence of unusual graves, we twenty-first-century folks can connect to the love and loss of others a long time ago. Our twenty-first-century tools also help us to pay tribute in ways no one could have dreamed of fifty years ago.

DUOS LOCKED IN TIME

Imagine a small village, complete with a lake, all sheltered by a cave near the sea. What could go on there? Folks trading for goods. Families raising their kids. Everyone waiting for the next attack. Or the next good thing. The cycle of birth, life, and death, over and over again.

There was such a cave in the very southern part of Greece, named Alepotrypa, "Foxhole." It is big and it is roomy; the cave is 300 meters (320 yards) deep, 60 meters (65 yards) high, and 100 meters (109 yards) wide—big enough for an American football game.

Below that cave was a second one, with a river about three hundred yards (two hundred seventy meters) long. From what we know, the cave was home, workplace, and burial ground for three thousand years. Not all at once, most likely; people came and went from about 6000 to 3200 BCE.

The spot reminds us of another cave in the land of legend, says Dr. Michael Galaty, now a professor of anthropology at the University of Michigan. "If you've ever seen *The Lord of the Rings*, this might make you recall the mines of Moria— the cave is really that impressive."

The River Styx from Greek myths comes to mind, as well, thanks to that second cave and its underground river. Was it the domain of Hades, Greek god of the underworld?

Then about 3000 BCE the cave caved in, from an earth-quake perhaps. It stayed silent until 1958, and in 1970 exca-vation began. Bones in the cave, burials aplenty, started to tell the world its secrets.

There were the remains of at least one hundred sev-enty people surrounded by a host of ceramic pots, beads of agate, ivory, and stone and metal tools. Giorgos

A male and female are tucked together in a single grave in Greece's Alepotrypa cave.

Papathanassopoulos, the Greek archaeologist who directed the exploration at Foxhole, was said to think that area residents had honored the site as a place to deposit their dead. About thirty percent of their craniums, or skulls, show signs of blunt force trauma. It seems they lived and died in violent times.

On a terrace of land above the cave's entrance appeared three sets of double burials. One housed a child and a baby, and the next was the grave of a young man and woman curled up and facing each other. Not until 2015 did the third grave emerge from the earth, possibly Greece's most dramatic and oldest grave ever discovered.

Within it a man and a woman had been buried as one. DNA tests worked their wonder on the young couple, revealing that they were between twenty-three and twenty-five years old. Their bones showed no signs of violent death. But died they did, either in each other's arms, or arranged that way by other human hands. Anastasia Papathanasiou, a Greek archaeologist who had long worked at Alepotrypa, offered her take on the burial. "It's a very natural hug; it doesn't look like they were arranged in this posture at a much later date."

Could it be that these Neolithic, late–Stone Age people, created a burial ground in that cave that morphed into the underworld of Greek myths? Dr. Galaty thinks so. "The burial sites and rituals that took place really do give the cave an underworld feel. It's like Hades, complete with its own River Styx."

Back in 2007 archaeologists had found another Neolithic couple. At that time they thought that they were the first to discover the world's oldest example of embracing lovers. This tomb lay in San Giorgio, Italy, near the city of Mantua. Rather than excavate the couple bone by bone, the lead archaeologist decided to remove the entire grave in one piece. "We want to keep them just as they have been all this time—together," explained Elena Menotti.

Italians nicknamed the pair "Lovers of Valdaro," although, of course, no one can be sure if this was a love-locked duo at all. Researchers did make the call that one was female and the other one male. They were young, between eighteen and twenty, and about five feet two inches (1.6 meters) tall.

The "lovers" were seemingly buried with loving hands, because they were sent to the afterlife with grave goods. A flint arrowhead lay near the male's head, while the female rated three tools: a long blade beside her thigh, and two

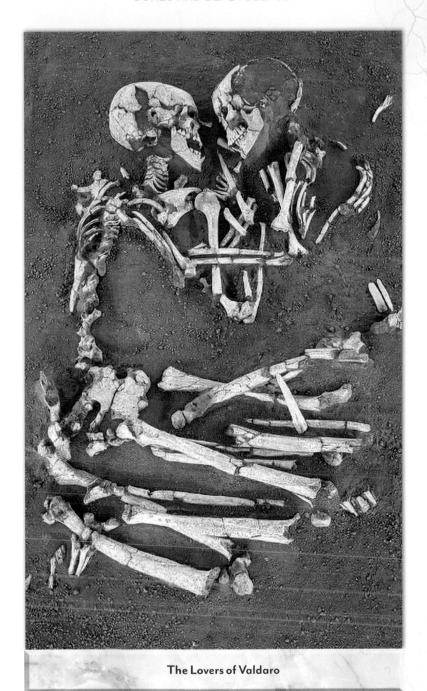

The Lovers of Valdaro

other knives under her pelvis. Whether for work or for defense, she seems to have been well-equipped.

The Lovers of Valdaro now have a new resting place in the National Archaeological Museum of Mantua.

A much newer example of a loving pair caught experts off guard in 2013, when they appeared during an excavation of an old Roman Catholic monastery in Romania. A hand-holding couple had been laid to rest there, sometime between 1450 and 1550.

The male had a broken hip (or sternum, depending on which source you read), but the female's bones seemed to be perfect. That raised the question—had the woman ended her life to join her lover in the grave? Did she play Juliet to her Romeo, as William Shakespeare later wrote in his famous play?

That wouldn't have happened, explained the archaeologist in charge. Taking of one's own life was thought to be a mortal sin at that time, and thus the couple would not have been buried in holy ground.

We can wonder, then, whether the woman died of a broken heart.

COMING HOME FROM THE *OKLAHOMA*

Every year on December 7 news media and many families look at the date and remember. December 7 marks the sneak attack by air and sea by the Empire of Japan on the Pacific Fleet of the U.S. Navy in 1941. A "day that will live in infamy," said President Franklin D. Roosevelt to the nation the day after. The president asked Congress to declare war on Japan, and the United States entered World War II.

The American fleet, four battleships and assorted other navy vessels, was docked at Pearl Harbor in Hawaii. Two aircraft carriers were at sea.

Hardest hit was the USS *Arizona*, which exploded and sank after Japanese bombs struck it. More than eleven hundred men lie in that sunken battleship, now a tomb for the dead. A memorial floats above. When you visit, you can see tiny bubbles of oil as they continue to leak from the ship. After all this time. To think that beneath your feet are the bones of so many dead is very sobering.

Docked nearby was the USS *Oklahoma*, another battleship manned by thirteen hundred navy sailors and seventy-seven marines. It was Sunday morning, and all was quiet. The *Oklahoma*'s band was preparing to strike up some tunes for a morning ceremony. Just before eight o'clock, airplanes darkened the sky, and the call "Air Raid" sounded from the PA system.

Eight Japanese torpedoes pierced the *Oklahoma* and blew it open. The massive ship rolled over and sank, masts down, into the harbor bottom. It took only ten minutes.

Hundreds escaped the calamity, but hundreds more were trapped inside the *Oklahoma*'s metal hull. A lucky few escaped when rescuers cut through the hull and got them to

The USS *Oklahoma* capsized at Pearl Harbor on December 7, 1941.

safety. But the rest of the young men, who came from towns large and small, couldn't get out, and they drowned. Their bodies remained in the ship for more than a year. They decomposed and turned into bones—soaked in the fuel oil on board the ship. Seawater in the hull stirred them around.

Officially, the remains became "unknowns," unidentified sailors and marines. In the 1940s, only dental records could help with the process of putting a name to a skull or even a jaw.

The *Oklahoma* was salvaged and turned upright in 1943. The dead were placed in multiple caskets in graves in two cemeteries. In 1947 the navy exhumed them, with the plan to rebury them in the National Memorial Cemetery of the Pacific (the NMCP) in the "Punchbowl," a volcanic valley in Honolulu. About twenty-seven individuals were identified at that time.

Someone made the strange decision to organize the remains according to the bones: all leg bones, for example, or all arm bones or skulls. But a navy official decided that comingling the bones was wrong and ordered that they be arranged as skeletons. No matter that each skeleton was itself comingled, a mix of bones from different men. By 1950 about four

The USS *Oklahoma* was salvaged and turned upright in 1943.

hundred unknowns were buried in the NMCP. Their remains filled sixty-two caskets.

For many years the U.S. military held to a rule that graves of the dead, once formally buried, should *never* be disturbed. That held true for the *Oklahoma*'s men buried in the Punchbowl. Their names were engraved on a memorial tablet, a common solution to remember them and a place of reflection for their families and others.

And yet this practice left someone uneasy. He was Mr. Ray Emory, once a sailor who had lived through the horror of that Sunday morning attack and never forgot those who died. Emory lived on Oahu, the island home to Honolulu and Pearl Harbor. He went walking through the Punchbowl, read grave markers, and started his own investigation.

Emory, a mechanical engineer, added a second job to his résumé: amateur historian. He had targeted the burial of a

The United States Navy surprised Ray
Emory with an honor ceremony in 2018.

single sailor and had big doubts about the written records
on his remains. It took him quite some time to convince the
navy to have them tested.

The *Washington Post* reported:

In 2003 researcher and Pearl Harbor survivor Ray
Emory, now 94, used files he unearthed in the
National Archives about one Oklahoma sailor to
get officials to dig up a casket believed to contain
his remains.

That sailor, Ensign Eldon Wyman, was duly
identified, along with four others whose remains
were in the casket. But extensive DNA testing
revealed that there were also remnants of 90
additional people in the caskct.

Emory had opened the door to possibilities. DNA testing could help identify those masses of human remains from the *Oklahoma*.

By 2015, with DNA testing now helping families find each other, it made sense for the U.S. military to update its own policy on the "unknowns." The Defense POW/MIA Accounting Agency was tasked with the job, taking on the remains from the *Oklahoma* as it has for unidentified prisoners of war and those missing in action from wars in Korea, Vietnam, and more.

The bones of the *Oklahoma* men were sent to two laboratories for study. Sets of the lower remains were airlifted to Offutt Air Force Base in Nebraska, but the skulls stayed in Hawaii, where experts worked with DNA extracted from teeth.

There was a huge amount of work to do. Old sets of files were retrieved and studied. Dental x-rays and chest x-rays from the living would now help to identify the dead. The navy looked for families of the dead and collected DNA samples from them.

There were thirteen thousand bones open to study. One of the caskets held the remains of nearly one hundred men. Twelve bones from one man, once tested, were found to have come from eleven separate caskets.

The team in Nebraska developed two new ways to identify individual men from this mixed-up assortment of bones. One is a database they named "CoRA," Commingled

Remains Analytics. The other is "automated osteometric sorting." Osteo—bones, and metric—measurement.

They use computer programs to compare bones based on their size and shape, and then which bones fit together in joints. "If you have someone who is very short and someone who is very tall, you can separate them out using osteometric sorting," explained Dr. Carrie Brown. She is a forensic anthropologist and leads the team at the Nebraska lab. Dr. Brown welcomed the challenge of trying to ID the remains.

It's powerful that a nation is still doing this type of challenging and difficult endeavor to bring home guys after seventy-six years, and it's work we're still doing. It's a promise that we're making as a nation to individuals that serve that [we] will bring you home, and if anything should happen to you we will return you to your own soil . . . It's important.

By 2019 about three hundred fifteen sets of remains had been identified and returned to their families. Those were the "easy" cases. There were another one hundred fifty sets of remains still to identify. Moreover, the agency had not found "family reference samples" for fifty-two of the dead.

🏛 🏛 🏛

Is this kind of work worth the time? Is it worth the expense? Angry letters to the editor of the *New York Times*, for example, called out the U.S. military for spending so much money to build its new forensic lab in Hawaii. A waste, some wrote. The dead should stay where they are, wrote others.

Navy Fireman Second Class George C. Ford

But in the summer of 2018, the body of Navy Fireman Second Class George C. Ford, twenty-five, from Carroll, Nebraska, made its final journey from the lab on Offutt Air Force Base to the cemetery where his parents are buried. "At first I was just shocked to know that somebody cared enough to keep researching," Rhonda Maurer, George Ford's grandniece, told a reporter in 2018. "It's just been exciting. And really unbelievable."

Navy Storekeeper Second Class Gerald Lee Clayton

In another part of Nebraska, the family of Navy Storekeeper Second Class Gerald Lee Clayton, twenty-one, of Central City, gathered to welcome him home for burial.

Gerald Clayton's cousin and best friend, Bob Clayton, was killed at Pearl Harbor that same day. Bob Clayton still rests in the USS *Arizona*.

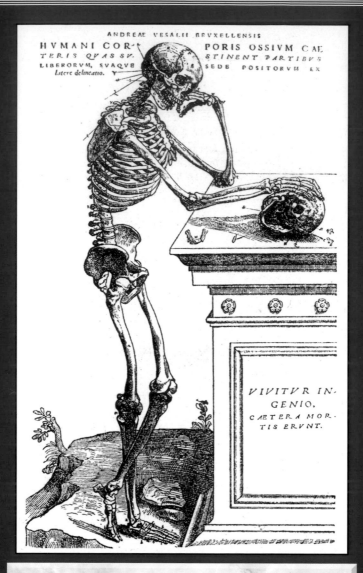

This skeleton gazing on a skull appeared in 1543 in the book *De humani corporis fabrica libri septem* (*Seven books on the fabric of the human body*.) Its author was Andreas Vesalius, the founder of modern anatomy. Translation of Latin inscription on the pedestal: *Vivitur Ingenio, Caetera Mortis Erunt / Genius Lives On, All Else Will Die.*

AFTERWORD

DID READING THIS BOOK CREEP YOU OUT?

After writing it and looking at so many facial reconstructions of skulls like that of King Richard III, I confess that when I look at other living people, sometimes I wonder what their skulls look like!

Looking at the bones of people who have gone before us and learning their stories can be rather unsettling. But there is a truth behind them about human nature, which you will learn as you grow up.

In my first Creepy and True book, *Mummies Exposed!*, I wrote that there is always something new to learn about something old. Sometimes archaeologists and anthropologists offer their ideas about the buried bones in a site, and years later, other experts revisit the boney remains and decide something else. The Neanderthal flower burials are a perfect example.

I often talk about the huge amount of research that's the foundation of books like these in the Creepy and True series. Like most nonfiction writers, I say that investigating my topic is the fun part of my work! For instance, for each set of bones I wrote about for this book, I started by reading the old research about their discovery and what the experts theorized about it. Next I turned to newer research and learned about that, too.

I let all of that roll around in my mind awhile. Then I boil all of that information "down to the bones" and write it in a way that I hope will capture your imagination.

When all is said and done for the first draft, I have put about forty thousand words on the page, which is about ten percent of what I have learned. Picture an iceberg: This book is only the tip of the iceberg and underneath the other ninety percent is all research.

When I was in school, our resources were hard copies of library books, magazines, newspapers, and encyclopedias on the shelf. Today you have the great privilege of being able to log on to the Internet and look for what you want to learn.

I would warn you, however, that what you find is not always true. There's way too much outdated information out there. Sometimes there are honest mistakes (I know because I have made them myself!). Then there's other stuff on the Internet and social media that's plainly dishonest . . . which I find *totally creepy and NOT true.*

Like the experts who dig for bones and then study them, you must conduct *your* research in a careful way. To help you figure this out, you can ask a media specialist at school, your teachers, or the librarians at your public library. And you can ask for help from adults like me who poke around the Web and see what's truc and what is *not*.

The author George R. R. Martin said this:

"The truth is in our bones, for flesh decays and bone endures."

The bones of an ancient six-year-old child found during an archaeological excavation

NOTES

CHAPTER ONE: DIGGING ON THE BONES OF A KING

6   "When you're writing a screenplay": Maev Kennedy, "It's like Richard III wanted to be found." *Guardian,* February 5, 2013. See www.theguardian .com/uk/2013/feb/05/king-richard-iii-found.

9   "[Two] walls . . . match up, meaning that the human remains": "The Discovery of Richard III: Saturday, 1 September 2012," University of Leicester, Archaeology. See www.le.ac.uk/richardiii /archaeology/1september.html.

10   "We excavated his legs up to his pelvis": Turi King, comment to the author, September 28, 2020.

13   "It's considered . . . reverence": *Richard II: The Archaeological Dig.* University of Leicester. See www.le.ac.uk/richardiii/multimedia/videos /archaeologicaldig.html.

14   "there were several glancing blows really from a sharp implement": Jo Appleby, "The Discovery of Richard III: Injuries to the Remains," University of Leicester. See www.le.ac.uk/richardiii/multimedia/videos /injuriestoremains.html.

14   "[Henry] was able to show": Turi King, "The Discovery of Richard III: Removing a Tooth for DNA Analysis," University of Leicester. See www.le.ac.uk/richardiii/multimedia/videos/removingtooth.html.

16   "You grind up the sample into a powder": "The Discovery of Richard III: Identifying the Remains." University of Leicester. See www.le.ac.uk /richardiii/multimedia/videos/identifyingremains.html.

17   "Now what you're hoping is that at the end of this process": Ibid.

19   "Ladies and gentlemen": "The Discovery of Richard III: The Scientific Outcome" (press conference, February 4, 2013), University of Leicester. See www.le.ac.uk/richardiii/multimedia/videos/pressconference.html.

CHAPTER TWO: STONES AND BONES . . . KRAKATOA AND TAMBORA

23   "About the third week in July 1884, the boys": Simon Winchester, *Krakatoa: The Day the World Exploded: August 27, 1883* (New York: Harper Collins, 2003) 295.

24   "Welded thickly on to the rock's upper surface": Ibid., 296.

27   "And now tidings of disaster began to come thick and fast": D. K.,

"The Krakatoa Eruption," *New York Times*, October 22, 1883, 5. See timesmachine.nytimes.com/timesmachine/1883/10/22/106131363 .pdf?pdf_redirect=true&ip=0.

29   "Many of the 12,500 victims in Sumatra": R. A. van Sandick, *In the Realm of the Volcano* (Zutphen, Netherlands: W. J. Thieme & Cie, 1890). See www.vansandick.com/familie/archief/In_het_Rijk_van_Vulcaan/4 .php?lang=nl.

30   "this immense chain of volcanic mountains": Monique R. Morgan, "The Eruption of Krakatoa (also known as Krakatau) in 1883." See www .branchcollective.org/?ps_articles=monique-morgan-the-eruption-of -krakatoa-also-known-as-krakatau-in-1883.

30   "The first terse signal": Simon Winchester, "Nature's Way." *Guardian*, January 3, 2005. See www.theguardian.com/world/2005/jan/04 /indonesia.naturaldisasters.

30   "A remarkable atmospheric phenomenon," "great brilliancy," "afterglow": *Science*, January 1884, vol. III, no. 49, 38.

31   "Clouds like blood and tongues of fire": Allison Meier, "Clouds Like Blood: How a 19th-Century Volcano Changed the Color of Sunsets," *Hyperallergic*, January 9, 2015. See hyperallergic.com/173597/clouds -like-blood-how-a-19th-century-volcano-changed the-color-of -sunsets.

36   "when April, May, and the principal part of June, had passed": Carly Hilts, "London's Volcanic Winter," *Current Archaeology*, August 6, 2012. See www.archaeology.co.uk/articles/features/londons-volcanic-winter .htm.

37   "This past summer and fall have been so cold": "1810–1819 Timeline of Allen County, Indiana," *Allen County, Indiana Genealogy*. See www.acgsi org/genweb/county/timeline/1810s-timeline-of-allen-county-indiana .html.

40   "About 7 P.M. on the 10th of April [1815], three distinct columns": Bernice de Jong Boers, "Mount Tambora in 1815: A Volcanic Eruption in Indonesia and Its Aftermath," *Cornell University Press*, October 1995, No. 60, 40. See ecommons.cornell.edu/bitstream/handle/1813/54071 /INDO_60_0_1106964018_37_59.pdf?sequence=1&isAllowed=y.

40   "In the part of Saugur adjoining Tomboro, its effects": Ibid.

41   "She was knocked over on her back by the force of the pyroclastic flow": "Culture Destroyed by 1815 Volcano Rediscovered," Christopher Joyce, NPR: *All Things Considered*, February 28, 2006. See www.npr

.org/templates/ story/story.php?storyId=5237808#:~:text=Culture%20
Destroyed%20by%201815%20Volcano%20Rediscovered%20%3A%20
NPR&text=Culture%20Destroyed%20by%201815%20Volcano%2
-0Rediscovered%20The%20explosion%20in%201815,of%20the%20
village%20have%20surfaced.

41   "Pyroclastic flow is rather like a snow avalanche": Ibid.

45   "we've got lots of time. It's taken three hundred years": Ibid.

CHAPTER THREE. DE-ICING THE FRANKLIN EXPEDITION–DOWN TO THE BONES

50   "They were finding stuff": Joe O'Connor, "Inuit oral historian had
      'critical role' in solving mystery of doomed Franklin expedition."
      National Post, March 29, 2018. See nationalpost.com/news/inuit-oral
      -historian-had-critical-role-in-solving-mystery-of-doomed-franklin
      -expedition.

51   "Going back to her time": Ibid.

54   "Repulse Bay, July 29 Sir,—I have the honor to mention": Dr. John Rae,
      Sir Robert John Le Mesurier McClure, *The Melancholy Fate of Sir John
      Franklin and His Party, As Disclosed in Dr. Rae's Report; Together with the
      Despatches and Letters of Captain M'Clure, and Other Officers Employed in
      the Arctic Expeditions* (London, John Betts, 1854) iii–iv. See archive.org
      /stream/melancholyfateof00raej#page/n9/mode/2up.

55   "a party of 'white men,' amounting to about forty": Ibid.

55   "At a later date the same season": Ibid.

56   "From the mutilated state of many of the corpses": Ibid.

58   "I do not think of any of them had ever seen white people alive": Paul
      Watson, *Ice Ghosts: The Epic Hunt for the Lost Franklin Expedition* (New
      York: W. W. Norton & Company, 2017) 166.

58   "She said many of the white men dropped by the way": Ibid., 167.

58   "north extreme of King Williams's Land": "McClintock reports finding
      the Cairn and Bodies (January 1860)," *Canadian Mysteries.* See www
      .canadianmysteries.ca/sites/franklin
      /archive/text/McClintockFox_en.htm.

59   "Within a month after Lieutenant Gore placed the record": Ibid.

60   "a mere accumulation of deadweight": Watson, 169.

60   "The language of this people is peculiar to themselves." Charles Francis
      Hall, *Arctic Researches and Life Among the Esquimaux [microform]: Being
      the Narrative of an Expedition in Search of Sir John Franklin, in the Years
      1860, 1861, and 1862* (New York: Harper, 1866) 576.

61 "to search after such things as they could find": "The Franklin Mystery: Life & Death in the Artic," *Canada Mysteries*. See .wwwcanadianmysteries.ca/sites/franklin/archive/text /HallInnookpoozheejook1_en.htm.

61 "Question. What particular time of the year was it?" Ibid.

62 "one whole skeleton with clothes on": Ibid.

63 "All 105 men who set out for the Back River perished", Douglas R. Stenton, "Finding the Dead: Bodies, Bones and Burials from the 1845 Franklin Northwest Passage Expedition," *Polar Record*, vol. 54, no. 3 (Cambridge University Press, May 2018) 197–212. See doi.org/10.1017 /S0032247418000359.

CHAPTER FOUR: THE CALAMITY OF JANE

69 "famine beginning to look ghastly and pale in every face": "JAMESTOWN: 1609–10: STARVING TIME," London: 1624 Excerpts, National Humanities Center. See nationalhumanitiescenter .org/pds/amerbegin/settlement/text2/JamestownPercyRelation.pdf.

70 "Now whether she was better roasted": Rachel B. Herrmann, "The 'tragicall Historie': Cannibalism and Abundance in Colonial Jamestown." *William and Mary Quarterly*, vol. 68, no. 1 (2011): 47–74. See doi. org/10.5309/willmaryquar.68.1.0047 (accessed November 4, 2020).

77 "The chops to the forehead are very tentative, very incomplete": Joseph Stromberg, "Starving Settlers in Jamestown Colony Resorted to Cannibalism" *Smithsonian Magazine*, April 30, 2013. See www .smithsonianmag.com/history/starving-settlers-in-jamestown-colony -resorted-to-cannibalism-46000815/#8HoLAboTo4yow5vf.99.

79 "Our story became world famous because of how we survived": Dr. Roberto Canessa and Pablo Vierci. *I Had to Survive; How a Plane Crash in the Andes Inspired My Calling to Save Lives* (New York: Atria Books, 2016) 26.

80 "The days I'd spent away from the Fairchild had given me perspective": Nando Parrado and Vince Rause, *Miracle in the Andes: 72 Days on the Mountain and My Long Trek Home* (New York: Crown Publishers, 2006) 198–199.

CHAPTER FIVE: BENJAMIN FRANKLIN'S BASEMENT BONEYARD

86 "Here for example is a femur": "Ben Franklin's Bones," PBS, *Secrets of the Dead*. See www.pbs.org/wnet/secrets/api/ajax/?template=ajax-printable&id=2074.

90 "Most physicians don't cut into a body": Matt McCall, "The Secret Lives of Cadavers," *National Geographic,* July 29, 2016. See www .nationalgeographic.com/news/2016/07/body-donation-cadavers -anatomy-medical-education.

92 "Especially among dignitaries dying far from home": Mia Korpiola and Anu Lahtinen, eds., *Cultures of Death and Dying in Medieval and Early Modern Europe; An Introduction* (Helsinki: Helsinki Collegium for Advanced Studies University of Helsinki, 2015) 20. See www.helsinki .fi/collegium/journal/volumes/volume_18/Death%20and%20Dying %20in%20Medieval%20and%20Early%20Modern%20Europe.pdf.

92 "The strongest possible expressions were used to condemn": "The Development of Medical Museums in the Antebellum American South: Slave Bodies in Networks of Anatomical Exchange." *Bulletin of the History of Medicine* vol. 87, no. 1, Spring 2013, 32–62. See doi .org/10.1353/bhm.2013.0016.

96 "Our whole scientific team has a deep respect for these individuals": Malcolm X. Abram, "Robert L. Blakely, 52, GSU associate professor of anthropology," *Atlanta Constitution,* 22 September 22, 1997, 62. See www.newspapers.com/clip/39498971/obituary-robert-l-blakely.

98 "a minimum of forty-four adults (individuals fifteen years and older) and nine children (ages fourteen years and younger)": D. W. Owsley, K. S. Bruwelheide, R. L. Jantz, J. L. Koste, M. Outlaw, "Skeletal Evidence of Anatomical and Surgical Training in Nineteenth-Century Richmond" in Kenneth C. Nystrom K., ed., *The Bioarchaeology of Dissection and Autopsy in the United States* (New York: Springer, 2017) 143–164.

99 "[This particular grave robbery] was done": Christina J. Hodge, "Non-Bodies of Knowledge: Anatomized Remains from the Holden Chapel Collection, Harvard University." *Journal of Social Archaeology*, February 4, 2013, 17, cited in Dolly Stolze. "Bodies in the Basement: The Forgotten Stolen Bones of America's Medical Schools," *Atlas Obscura,* January 22, 2015. See www.atlasobscura.com/articles/bodies-in-the-basement-the -forgotten-bones-of-america-s-medical-schools.

100 "During the past few days the citizens of North Bend": "HUMAN HYENAS: Hon. John Scott Harrison Torn From His Grave." *Cincinnati Enquirer*, May 31, 1878, 8. See search.proquest.com.research .cincinnatilibrary.org/hnpcincinnatienquirershell/results /B8DE191423CB4675PQ/1?accountid=39387.

101 "sensation . . . stiff": Ibid.

101 "In the cellar they found first a huge 'chute'": Ibid.
103 "It was taut ... 'Here is somebody'": Ibid.
103 "It is not the man": Ibid.
104 "Still Mr. Harrison was silent": Ibid.

CHAPTER SIX: HUMAN OFFERINGS HERE, THERE, AND EVERYWHERE . . .

109 "A world of information": Lizzie Wade, "Feeding the gods: Hundreds of skulls reveal massive scale of human sacrifice in Aztec capital," *Science*, June 21, 2018. See www.sciencemag.org/news/2018/06/feeding-gods-hundreds-skulls-reveal-massive-scale-human-sacrifice-aztec-capital.

109 "It is important to understand the worldview of the Aztecs": James Fredrick, "500 Years Later, The Spanish Conquest of Mexico Is Still Being Debated," NPR, *Weekend Edition Sunday*, November 10, 2019. See www.npr.org/2019/11/10/777220132/500-years-later-the-spanish-conquest-of-mexico-is-still-being-debated.

113 "disarticulated and rarely associated with burial goods": Ying Meng, An Archaeological Investigation of Human Sacrifice at Xibeigang in Anyang During the Late Shang Dynasty" (master's thesis, The University of British Columbia, Vancouver, November 2009) 10.

119 "The excavation was made because the place was planned for modern house building": Ove Hemmendorf, email to the author, October 18, 2020.

123 "They [human beings] constituted the ultimate sacrifice": Charlotte Persson, "Child Sacrifice and Other Viking Activities," Real Clear Science, December 1, 2014. See www.realclearscience.com/articles/2014/12/02/child_sacrifice_and_other_viking_activities_108967.html.

CHAPTER SEVEN: BATTLES OF THE BONES AND OTHER THINGS

126 "Hominid—the group consisting of all modern and extinct Great Apes": Beth Blaxland, "Hominid and hominin—what's the difference?" *Australian Museum*, February 10, 2020. See australian.museum/learn/science/human-evolution/hominid-and-hominin-whats-the-difference.

131 "Meanwhile, Johanson turns to the camera to begin an explanation": Roger Lewin, *Bones of Contention: Controversies in the Search for Human Origins* (Chicago: University of Chicago Press, 1987) 17.

133 "I think if we can make it understood": "Human Evolution and Why It Matters: A Conversation with Leakey and Johanson." *American Museum of Natural History*, May 9, 2011. See www.youtube.com/watch?v=pBZ8o-lmAsg.

134 "CRADLE OF HUMANKIND, South Africa—Nine-year-old Matthew Berger": Celia W. Dugger and John Noble Wilford, "New Hominid Species Discovered in South Africa," *New York Times* archive, April 8, 2010. See archive.nytimes.com/www.nytimes.com/2010/04/09 /science/09fossil.html.

135 "It's almost the entire top half of a body . . . as well": University of Cambridge, "Discovery at 'flower burial' site could unravel mystery of Neanderthal death rites," *Science Daily*, February 18, 2020. See www .sciencedaily.com/releases/2020/02/200218073450.htm.

137 "gross deforming osteoarthritis": "What does it mean to be human?" *Smithsonian Museum of Natural History*. See humanorigins.si.edu /evidence/human-fossils/fossils/la-chapelle-aux-saints.

138 "In fact, the project never set out to find more bones": Emma Pomeroy in a comment to the author, October 19, 2020.

139 "The new excavation suggests that some of these bodies": *Science Daily*. See www.sciencedaily.com/releases/2020/02/200218073450.htm.

141 "One tough dude": Douglas Preston, "The Kennewick Man Finally Freed to Share His Secrets," *Smithsonian Magazine*, September 2014. See www.smithsonianmag.com/history/kennewick-man-finally-freed -share-his-secrets-180952462/?all.

145 "It was inspiring to see so many different people, from different walks of life come to appreciate": Terry Fifield, "Shuká Káa," email to the author, October 6, 2020.

146 What to Do If You Find Human Bones: Terry Fifield, email to the author, October 9, 2020.

148 "Over millions of years, water in the nearby rocks": "Dinosaur Bones," *American Museum of Natural History*. See www.amnh.org/dinosaurs /dinosaur-bones.

CHAPTER EIGHT: SHAFTED

149 "Here we report the earliest evidence of lethal interpersonal violence": Nohemi Sala et al, "Lethal Interpersonal Violence in the Middle Pleistocene," PLoS One, May 2015, vol.10 no. 5. See doi.org/e0126589, www.ncbi.nlm.nih.gov/pmc/articles/PMC4446311.

153 "Accidental or unintentional trauma typically affects the sides of the cranial vault": Ibid.

153 "Based on the absence of cut marks": Ibid.

154 "deliberate, lethal interpersonal aggression in the hominin fossil record": Ibid.

159 "the broken lenses of the Empress's eyeglasses": Edmund Walsh, "The Last Days of the Romanovs," *Atlantic*, March 1928. See www.theatlantic .com/magazine/toc/1928/03.

164 "Prohibitions . . . a bit of discipline never hurt anyone!" Les Catacombes de Paris. See www.catacombes.paris.fr/en/visit/read-your-visit.

CHAPTER NINE: BONES AND BENEVOLENCE

166 "If you've ever seen *The Lord of the Rings*": Charles Q. Choi, "Killer Cave May Have Inspired Myth of Hades," *Live Science*, November 28, 2012. See www.livescience.com/25091-greek-hades-cave-burial.html.

168 "The burial sites and rituals that took place": Ibid.

168 "It's a very natural hug . . . date": Nick Romeo, "Embracing Stone Age Couple Found in Greek Cave." *National Geographic,* February 20, 2015. See www.nationalgeographic.com/history/article/150220 embracing -skeletons-greece- diros-alepotrypa-cave- archaeology.

168 "We want to keep them just as they have been all this time": Phil Stewart, "Scientists to save 5,000-year-old embrace," Reuters: Science & Space, February 14, 2007. See www.reuters.com/article/us-italy-embrace /scientists-to-save-5000-year-old-embrace-idUSL12831255020070214.

174 "In 2003 researcher and Pearl Harbor survivor Ray Emory": Michael E. Ruane, "After 74 years, bones from Pearl Harbor tomb ship may be identified," *Washington Post*, December 6, 2015. See www .washingtonpost.com/local/after-74-years-bones-from-pearl-harbor -tomb-ship-may-be-identified/2015/12/06/60263b86-8ee7-11e5-acff -673ae92ddd2b_story.html.

176 "It's powerful that a nation is still doing this type of challenging and difficult endeavor": Tracie Mauriello, "Seventy-six years after USS Oklahoma was torpedoed scientists work to return the fallen to their families," *Pittsburgh Post-Gazette,* December 7, 2017.

177 "At first I was . . . unbelievable": Steve Liewer, "Offutt lab has identified remains of 242 who died on USS Oklahoma. Now come the harder cases." *Daily Nonpareil,* December 31, 2019. See nonpareilonline.com /news/local/offutt-lab-has-identified-remains-of-who-died-on-uss /article_35254bfb-7c16-5d1c-81a5-8dad1716dd8e.html.

AFTERWORD

181 "The truth is in our bones, for flesh decays and bone endures": George R. R. Martin, *A Feast for Crows* (New York: Bantam, 2006). See www .goodreads.com/quotes/7611773-the-truth-is-in-our-bones-for-flesh -decays-and.

SELECT BIBLIOGRAPHY

CHAPTER ONE: DIGGING ON THE BONES OF A KING

Online Sources

"The Discovery of Richard III." University of Leicester. See www.le.ac.uk
/richardiii/index.html.

CHAPTER TWO: STONES AND BONES . . . KRAKATOA AND TAMBORA

Online Sources

van Sandick. R. A. *In the Realm of the Volcano.* September 1890. See www
.vansandick.com/familie/archief/In_het_Rijk_van_Vulcaan/4.php?lang=nl.

"What is a Volcano? *About Volcanoes.* Volcano Hazards Program. United
States Geological Survey. See www.usgs.gov/natural-hazards/volcano
-hazards/about-volcanoes.

Books

Winchester, Simon. *Krakatoa: The Day the World Exploded: August 27,
1883.* New York: HarperCollins, 2003.

CHAPTER THREE: DE-ICING THE FRANKLIN EXPEDITION—DOWN TO THE BONES

Online Sources

"McClintock reports finding the Cairn and Bodies (January 1860)." *Canadian
Mysteries.* See www.canadianmysteries.ca/sites/franklin/archive/text
/McClintockFox_en.htm.

O'Connor, Joe. "Inuit oral historian had 'critical role' in solving mystery of
doomed Franklin expedition." *National Post,* March 30, 2018. See
nationalpost.com/news/inuit-oral-historian-had-critical-role-in-solving
-mystery-of-doomed-franklin-expedition.

Rae, Dr. John and McClure, Sir Robert John Le Mesurier. *The Melancholy
Fate of Sir John Franklin and His Party, As Disclosed in Dr. Rae's Report;
Together with the Despatches and Letters of Captain M'Clure, and Other
Officers Employed in the Arctic Expeditions.* London: John Betts, 1854. See
archive.org/stream/melancholyfateof00raej#page/n9/mode/2up.

Stenton, Douglas R. "Finding the Dead: Bodies, Bones and Burials from the
1845 Franklin Northwest Passage Expedition." Cambridge University
Press, *Polar Record* 54, no. 3. See doi.org/10.1017/S0032247418000359.

Books

Watson, Paul. *Ice Ghosts: The Epic Hunt for the Lost Franklin Expedition.* New York: W. W. Norton & Company, 2017.

CHAPTER FOUR: THE CALAMITY OF JANE

Online Sources

JAMESTOWN: 1609–10: "STARVING TIME." London: 1624 Excerpts. National Humanities Center. See nationalhumanitiescenter.org/pds /amerbegin/settlement/text2/JamestownPercyRelation.pdf.

"Jane: A 'STARVING TIME' TRAGEDY." Jamestowne Rediscovery: *Historic Jamestowne.* See historicjamestowne.org/archaeology/jane.

Books

Canessa, Dr. Roberto and Vierci, Pablo. *I Had to Survive; How a Plane Crash in the Andes Inspired My Calling to Save Lives.* New York: Atria Books, 2016.

Parrado, Nando and Rause, Vince. *Miracle in the Andes: 72 Days on the Mountain and My Long Trek Home.* New York: Crown Publishers, 2006.

CHAPTER FIVE: BENJAMIN FRANKLIN'S BASEMENT BONEYARD

Online Sources

Benjamin Franklin House. See benjaminfranklinhouse.org.

Korpiola, Mia and Lahtinen, Anu, eds., *Cultures of Death and Dying in Medieval and Early Modern Europe: An Introduction.* Helsinki Collegium for Advanced Studies, University of Helsinki, 2015. See www.helsinki.fi /collegium/journal/volumes/volume_18/Death%20and%20Dying%20 in%20Medieval%20and%20Early%20Modern%20Europe.pdf.

McCall, Matt. "The Secret Lives of Cadavers." *National Geographic,* July 29, 2016. See www.nationalgeographic.com/news/2016/07/body -donation-cadavers-anatomy-medical-education.

CHAPTER SIX: HUMAN OFFERINGS HERE, THERE, AND EVERYWHERE . . .

Online sources

Lizzie Wade. "Feeding the gods: Hundreds of skulls reveal massive scale of human sacrifice in Aztec capital." *Science,* June 21, 2018. See www .sciencemag.org/news/2018/06/feeding-gods-hundreds-skulls-reveal -massive-scale-human-sacrifice-aztec-capital.

Books

Bremen, Adam of. *History of the Archbishops of Hamburg-Bremen.* New York: Columbia University Press, 1959.

CHAPTER SEVEN: BATTLES OF THE BONES AND OTHER THINGS
Online Sources

Blaxland, Beth. "Hominid and hominin—what's the difference?" *Australian Museum*, February 10, 2020. See australian.museum/learn/science /human-evolution/hominid-and-hominin-whats-the-difference.

"Discovery at 'flower burial' site could unravel mystery of Neanderthal death rites." *Science Daily*, February 18, 2020. See www.sciencedaily.com /releases/2020/02/200218073450.htm.

Dixon, Mim. "Shuká Kaa Is Given a Final Resting Place After 10,300 Years (Observations During the Ceremony: Sept. 25–27, 2008." U.S. Forest Service, U.S. Department of Agriculture, January 2009. See www.fs.usda .gov/Internet/FSE_DOCUMENTS/fseprd506870.pdf.

"Human Evolution and Why It Matters: A Conversation with Leakey and Johanson." *American Museum of Natural* History, May 9, 2011. See www .youtube.com/watch?v=pBZ8o-lmAsg.

Preston, Douglas. "The Kennewick Man Finally Freed to Share His Secrets." *Smithsonian Magazine,* September 2014. See www.smithsonianmag.com /history/kennewick-man-finally-freed-share-his-secrets-180952462/?all.

CHAPTER EIGHT: SHAFTED
Online Sources

Les Catacombes de Paris. See www.catacombes.paris.fr/en/visit/read-your -visit.

Sala, Nohemi et.al. "Lethal Interpersonal Violence in the Middle Pleistocene." PLoS One. May 27, 2015. See www.ncbi.nlm.nih.gov/pmc /articles/PMC4446311.

Walsh, Edmund. "The Last Days of the Romanovs." *Atlantic*, March 1928. See www.theatlantic.com/magazine/toc/1928/03.

CHAPTER NINE: BONES AND BENEVOLENCE
Online Sources

DPAA Public Affairs. "DPAA Makes 200th Identification from USS Oklahoma Unknown Remains." Defense POW/MIA Accounting Agency. See www.dpaa.mil.

Liewer, Steve. "Omaha forensic lab works to identify Pearl Harbor victims." *Omaha World-Herald,* January 26, 2016. See journalstar.com/ap/state /omaha-forensic-lab-works-to-identify-pearl-harbor-victims/article _40eca7a2-39a5-5f81-9eab-332e9414295f.html.

Olson, Wyatt, "Pearl Harbor survivor who led quest to identify USS
Oklahoma 'unknowns' dies." *Stars and Stripes,* August 20, 2018. See www
.stripes.com/news/pacific/pearl-harbor-survivor-who-led-quest-to-identify
-uss-oklahoma-unknowns-dies-1.543528.

Ruane, Michael E. "After 74 years, bones from Pearl Harbor tomb ship may
be identified." *Washington Post,* December 6, 2015. See www
.washingtonpost.com/local/after-74-years-bones-from-pearl-harbor-tomb
-ship-may-be-identified/2015/12/06/60263b86-8ee7-11e5-acff
-673ae92ddd2b_story.html.

GENERAL SOURCES

All states in the United States and many municipal governments have laws
relating to burials, cemeteries, and the discovery of human remains on public
and private lands. The statements above are common to most of those laws and
policies. Below is a sample of Internet sources on the subject.

Massachusetts Historical Commission
www.sec.state.ma.us/mhc/mhcpdf/knowhow4.pdf

National NAGPRA Program
(Native American Graves Protection and Repatriation Act)
www.nps.gov/orgs/1335/index.htm

Society for American Archaeology
www.saa.org/about-archaeology/archaeology-law-ethics

State of Alaska Office of History and Archaeology
dnr.alaska.gov/parks/oha/ahrs/remains.htm

Washington State Department of Archaeology and Historic Preservation
dahp.wa.gov/archaeology/human-remains/what-do-i-do if-ive-found-
human-remains

Wisconsin Historical Society
wisconsinhistory.org/Records/Article/CS3124

PICTURE CREDITS

Page iv: Hans Holbein the Younger, "Dance of Death," Art Institute of Chicago. **Page viii:** © National Portrait Gallery, London. **Pages 3, 157:** Library of Congress. **Pages 6, 10, 12, 16, 18:** University of Leicester. **Page 20:** John Everett Millais, "The Princes in the Tower," 1878; Royal Holloway and Bedford New College Art Collection. **Page 23:** The World Factbook 2020 (Washington, DC: Central Intelligence Agency, 2020). **Pages 25, 143, 151, 156:** Wikimedia Commons. **Page 29:** Welcome Collection. Attribution 4.0 International (CC BY 4.0). **Page 32:** National Museum of Norway. **Page 33:** Courtesy of Dr. Keith Kirk. **Page 34:** Earth Observatory, NASA. **Pages 35, 52, 133, 137, 156, 161, 162, 164:** Getty Images. **Page 38:** Courtesy of Rik Stoetman. **Page 42:** Veronika Pfeiffer/Alamy Stock Photo. **Page 45:** IanDagnall Computing/Alamy Stock Photo. **Page 47:** Universal Images Group North America LLC/Alamy Stock Photo. **Page 48:** Classic Image/Alamy Stock Photo. **Page 53:** Smurftrooper/Wikimedia Commons. **Page 53 (top):** Swanston, et al., "Franklin Expedition Lead Exposure: New Insights from High Resolution Confocal X-Ray Fluorescence Imaging of Skeletal Microstructure"; *PLOS ONE* (Public Library of Science), August 23, 2018. **Page 56:** INTERFOTO/Alamy Stock Photo. **Page 57:** The Miriam and Ira D. Wallach Division of Art, Prints, and Photographs: Picture Collection, New York Public Library ("The Franklin expedition—opening of the cairn on Point Victory which contained the record of Captains Croziee and Fitzjames," New York Public Library Digital Collections). **Page 61:** Album/Alamy Stock Photo. **Page 62:** Photo by W. Skinner/Royal Geographical Society via Getty Images. **Pages 63, 64 (top):** Douglas R. Stenton. Courtesy of the Government of Nunavut. **Page 64 (bottom):** Jason Fulford. **Page 68:** National Park Service. **Pages 72, 76:** Courtesy of Jamestown Rediscovery and Smithsonian Institution; Don Hurlbert, photographer. **Page 78:** Facial reconstruction contributors include Jiwoong Cheh, StudioEIS, Aimee Kratts; image courtesy of Jamestown. **Pages 80, 174:** Alamy Stock Photo. **Pages 81, 82, 107 (top):** AP Images. **Pages 84, 85, 87, 88:** Benjamin Franklin House. **Page 91:** Rebecca Hale. **Page 93:** National Center for Biotechnology Information. **Page 96:** Courtesy of the Historical Collections & Archives, Robert B. Greenblatt M.D. Library, Augusta University. **Page 98:** Hayward, Nathan. College scenes. [Boston] Mass.

ACKNOWLEDGMENTS

Writing this book has been an archaeological project of its own, as I searched for stories and sites to explore, excavated them for artifacts and evidence, and then returned to the exam room/laboratory in my head to distill what I'd learned and transform it into what you see here.

Thank you to my editor, Howard Reeves at Abrams Books for Young Readers, for helping me to rework and refine my thoughts and conclusions. There is always something new for me to learn about how to boil a manuscript down to the bones.

I so appreciate the experts and scholars who were so generous in answering my questions and helping me to get my facts in order. My thanks to Dr. Graeme Barker and Dr. Emma Pomeroy of the University of Cambridge for their assistance with photos and facts about the Shanidar burials. Thank you to Dr. Douglas Stenton of the University of Waterloo for his careful read of my draft and his photos from the Franklin expedition. A high school classmate, Dr. Keith Kirk, now retired from the USGS, helped me sort out volcanoes, tsunamis, and plate tectonics, as well as sharing his shot of a pumice raft. Dr. Turi King of the University of Leicester straightened me out about Richard III's DNA!

Terry Fifield, now retired from the U.S. Forest Service, spent much time sharing his experiences of the discovery and repatriation of Shuká Káa in Alaska, not to mention offering advice on what to do if you find bones in the wild.

To Jeff Ourvan, my agent at Jennifer Lyons Literary, I also say many thanks for pointing me to this project and offering his guidance in this ever-changing world of book writing.

Finally, my sincere thanks to my seventh-grade consultants on semantics and social studies, Cliff and Aarsh. You have so many exciting opportunities to discover and learn!

INDEX

Note: Page numbers in *italics* refer to illustrations.